GOD

SEEN THROUGH THE EYES
OF THE GREATEST MINDS

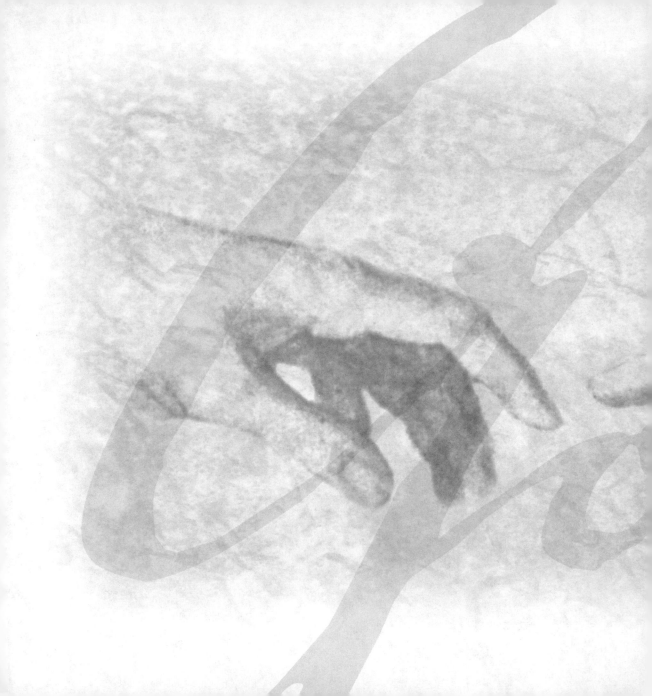

GOD

SEEN THROUGH THE EYES
OF THE GREATEST MINDS

MICHAEL CAPUTO

Our purpose at Howard Publishing is to:

- *Increase faith* in the hearts of growing Christians
- *Inspire holiness* in the lives of believers
- *Instill hope* in the hearts of struggling people everywhere

Because He's coming again!

God—Seen through the Eyes of the Greatest Minds
© 2000 by Michael Caputo
All rights reserved. Printed in the United States of America

Published by Howard Publishing Co., Inc.,
3117 North 7th Street, West Monroe, Louisiana 71291-2227

00 01 02 03 04 05 06 07 08 09   10 9 8 7 6 5 4 3 2 1

Library of Congress Cataloging-in-Publication Data
God : seen through the eyes of the greatest minds / [compiled by] Michael Caputo.
    p. cm.
  Includes bibliographical references (p.).
  ISBN 1-58229-132-2
    1. God—Quotations, maxims, etc. 2. Gifted persons—Quotations. I. Caputo, Michael, 1953–

BL205 .G637 2000
211—dc21   00-063233

Edited by Philis Boultinghouse
Interior design by LinDee Loveland
Portrait drawings by Katherine Cody Kicklighter

Scripture quoted from The Holy Bible, Authorized King James Version, © 1961 by The National Publishing Co.

DEDICATION

All pillars have a base. My base is my precious family.

My beautiful wife, Leonilda, who has been there, body and soul, for me and our children for many challenging years.

My precious children, Anthony, Julie, and Victor, who give meaning and excitement to my life.

My wonderful parents, Antonio and Teresa, who have molded me with much love. (Grazie mamma e papá per il vostro grande amore.)

My loving in-laws, Vittorio and Giulia Checca, who have given us much in many ways. (I vostri sacrifici non saranno dimenticati.)

My sister, Grace, and her children, Tony, Frank, Nino, and Lucy.

My Aunt Maria and uncles Rocco, Philip, and Domenic.

My brothers-in-law Greg and Nick, along with Nick's wife, Alba, Nonna Gina, and all my other relatives.

To them, and all my brothers and sisters in Christ in Italy and North America, I dedicate this work.

Each pillar and base rests upon a foundation. My sure foundation is the One this book is all about. To Him, "The All," I offer this small sacrifice. In His hands, may it become a blessing to many.

To *the* Highest God 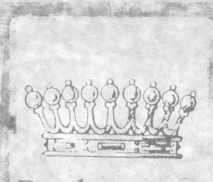 Be the

Glory

—Johann Sebastian Bach

CONTENTS

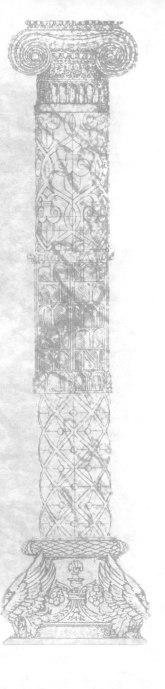

GREAT WRITERS *93*

ACKNOWLEDGMENTS

My deepest gratitude goes, first of all, to my forbearing wife and children, who have endured my obsession with a book that has taken years to research and complete. Thank you, Leonilda, Anthony, Julie, and Victor, for your love and patience.

Heartfelt appreciation to John Howard, president of Howard Publishing, for providing the opportunity for works such as mine to be published so as to edify and inspire the many who love their Creator. Special gratitude to Denny Boultinghouse, executive editor at Howard Publishing, for opening the door to the manuscript and to the managing editor, Philis Boultinghouse, a gracious and very supportive lady, for supervising the editing of this work with much patience and for her total committment to making this book worthy of the Almighty. My thanks, also, to Maxine Heath, production manager, for her invaluable help in understanding the foundational principles of copyright laws. Deep gratitude, also, to Lee Hankins, copyeditor, who has given this work countless hours of patient editing, and to two very talented ladies, Kathy Kicklighter, illustrator, and LinDee Loveland, graphic designer, who have made this work as attractive to the eye as it is to the intellect. Lastly, a special thank-you to a special Christian lady and a top translator, Renée Aviles, who was kind enough to help me translate some challenging and obscure French poetry.

Most of all, I would like to thank the Almighty, who inspired this work and who motivated me to carry on with the task the many times I felt tired and discouraged.

INTRODUCTION

This work finds its roots in a question that emerged in my mind many years ago and for which I sought an answer. The question was this: "Did great intellect and creativity lead brilliant men and women of the past to agnosticism or atheism, or did it lead them to believe in and submit to a Creator God?"

The search has been slow but very rewarding and enlightening. While you may not agree with all the views expressed by those quoted in this volume, you will find that most of the greatest men and women of the past were neither agnostics nor atheists. Most of them believed in God, and many made God the foundation of their lives. Surprisingly, belief in God was not always the result of intricate and time-consuming intellectual exercises, but it was, in many cases, the result of an intuitive experience. In fact, one can perceive in the writings of many great people a taking for granted of God's existence and a moving forward toward understanding His Great Mind.

To the great existential philosopher Sören Kierkegaard, trying to prove God's existence was "of all things most ridiculous."[1] Yet he believed in God. Kierkegaard believed that "the works of God are such that only God can perform them."[2] Sir Isaac Newton, centuries ago, saw God's presence and grandeur in nature. He held that humans may "come to the knowledge of the Deity...by the frame of nature."[3] Jean Jacques Rousseau saw God in "the blackboard of nature," wherein he saw "harmony and proportion."[4] Ralph Waldo Emerson saw in creation "a shadow of Him."[5]

Some great minds chose to block out any interest in God but did not succeed forever. Heinrich Heine discovered God at a late age: "In theology I must accuse myself of retrogression since I returned to the old superstition—a personal God."[6] The great impressionist painter Paul Cézanne stated that "once we have attained a great age we find no other support or consolation than in Religion."[7] The English poet Robert Browning temporarily chose to follow Shelley's example and adopted atheism. Later, he, too, returned to the belief in God and considered the existence of God "as certain beyond the need of proof."[8]

Belief in God has been an ennobling, energizing, and inspiring experience for many great men and women of genius. The great French painter Eugène Delacroix believed that "God's inner presence, beyond a doubt, constitutes the inspiration of men of genius."[9] The great composer Franz Liszt was convinced that "the Word of God reveals itself in the creations of genius."[10] The great Russian novelist Leo Tolstoy believed that "life is life, only when it is the carrying out of God's purpose."[11] Johann Sebastian Bach concluded most of his works with "Soli Deo Gloria" (To God alone be the glory).[12] The scientific giant Albert Einstein stated that the driving force behind his scientific search was "to know how God created this world.... I want to know His thoughts, the rest are details."[13]

What is also surprising is the number of great minds who adopted Christ as their Lord and Savior and who lived very devout Christian lives. Bach was a zealous

Lutheran.[14] Ludwig van Beethoven "ended his life as a true Christian."[15] Johann Goethe, toward the end of his life, affirmed that his love for "the founder of Christianity" could not be taken from him.[16] Johann Kepler rested on Christ's promise that Christians have awaiting them "faithful mansions in the house of the Father."[17] Rembrandt van Rijn was most probably a Mennonite.[18] Tolstoy was beyond any doubt a sincere and practicing Christian.[19] Dante Alighieri based his faith in his savior, Christ, "the door of our eternal dwelling."[20] To Franz Schubert, his Savior was "the glorious Christ."[21] William Shakespeare ended his life affirming his faith in the saving power of Jesus Christ.[22] Finally, the twentieth century's greatest philosopher, Ludwig Wittgenstein, expressed his faith in Christ as leading to salvation.[23]

Some might wrongly suggest that the luminaries quoted in this book are not from our "scientifically enlightened" times and that belief in God would not be found in great minds of the twentieth century. This assertion would be totally unfounded. The twentieth century had many great minds who believed in God. The scientific genius Einstein; the philosophical giants Wittgenstein, Henri Bergson, Pierre Teilhard de Chardin, and Simone Weil; the musical giants Igor Stravinsky, Gioacchino Antonio Rossini, Jean Sibelius, and Pietro Mascagni; the famed artist Pierre Auguste Renoir; the great literary geniuses T. S. Eliot, George Bernard Shaw, D. H. Lawrence, Luigi Pirandello, Grazia Deledda, Rainer Maria Rilke, and Alexander Solzhenitsyn are just some of the brilliant minds that lived in the twentieth century who held a firm belief in God.

In spite of a host of witnesses who shout otherwise, leading atheists have confidently asserted that intelligent, "enlightened minds" would never believe in a Creator. Their dogmatism may have intimidated and convinced others that this is indeed the case. This work is meant to give believers facts that tear down such assertions. As Francis Bacon wrote centuries ago, "It is little philosophy that inclines man's mind to atheism; but depth in philosophy brings about man's mind to religion."[24] The apostle Paul asserted with divine authority in Romans 1:19–20, "That which may be known of God is manifest in them; for God hath shewed it unto them. For the invisible things of him from the creation of the world are clearly seen, being understood by the things that are made, even his eternal power and Godhead; so that they are without excuse." No sound human reasoning can conclude that God does not exist. As most brilliant people of the past have concluded, it is the most evident of truths.

The people included in this work are most of the great luminaries who have shaped our civilization. Some are missing, either because material was not found or because they were either agnostics or atheists.

I have purposefully chosen to share my findings in quotation format rather than a long dissertation because I want the facts to speak for themselves without any interference from my interpretations. I also chose this approach to make available what I found to be missing: an extensive and well-documented collection of quotations on the most important subject there is. Lastly, I want this work to be a gathering of eminent voices that lift their praise to the greatest mind of all: the Author of all great minds and of all brilliance, the One to whom all of them owe their great intellect.

My hope is that this work will help many to see that, throughout the ages, brilliant minds have sought and found their Creator and that their belief in God has been for them an energizing, ennobling experience. Unlike what some atheists propagate, belief in God has not undermined the potential of humanity. On the contrary, it has been a fundamental and motivating factor behind many of humanity's greatest achievements.

The works of God are appreciated

Great ARTISTS

best by other creators.

—Leonardo da Vinci

BLAKE, *William*

It is God in all that is our companion and friend, for our God Himself says: "you are my brother, my sister and my mother."

Come, o Thou Lamb of God,
    and take away the remembrance of
Sin.
To sin and to hide the sin in sweet deceit is lovely!
To sin in the open face of day is cruel and pitiless!
But to record the sin for a reproach, to let the sun go down
To a remembrance of the sin, is a woe and horror,
A brooder of an evil day and a sun rising in blood!
Come then, O Lamb of God,
    and take away the remembrance of
Sin.

If God is anything He is understanding.

God is in the lowest effects as well as in the highest causes; for hc is become a worm that he may nourish the weak. For let it be remembered that creation is God descending according to the weakness of man, for our Lord is the word of God and every thing on earth is the word of God and its essence is God.

MAN MUST HAVE AND WILL HAVE SOME RELIGION: IF HE HAS NOT THE RELIGION OF JESUS, HE WILL HAVE THE RELIGION OF SATAN.

BUONARROTI, *Michelangelo*

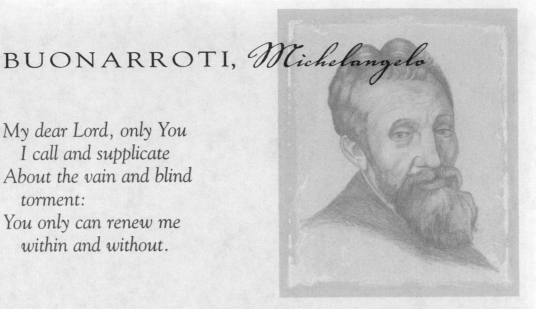

My dear Lord, only You
   I call and supplicate
About the vain and blind
   torment:
You only can renew me
   within and without.

Unless Thou show us Thine own true way
No man can find it; father! Thou must Lead.

Only You are the seed of pure and
   holy works,
That grow where You sow them
No one can follow You with his
   own worth
Except You show them Your holy
   ways.

Do not look with eyes of
   Justice upon my past…
May only Your blood touch
   and wash my faults
And evermore abound when
   I get old.

SONNET

I would love to want that which I do not want:

Between the fire and the heart of ice a veil is present

That quenches the fire, so that it prevents

The pen in its work, and makes the sheet a liar.

I love you with the tongue, and then I pain

That love does not reach the heart; nor do I know where

It opens the door to the mercy that enters

The heart, that casts out every merciless pride.

Tear the veil, my Lord, break down the wall

That with its hardness slows down

The brightness of your light, dark to the world!

Send the prophesied light so near to us

To your beautiful bride, that in my heart

I might burn without doubt, and only you believe.

By the cross, by Grace and by diverse trials I am sure... We will be in Heaven.

The vanities of life have taken from me the time to contemplate God.

CÉZANNE, *Paul*

I am helpless and can render you no service, but as I shall die before you [Emile Zola] I shall intercede before the Almighty for a good place for you.

Once we have attained a certain age we find no other support or consolation than in religion.

Let me repeat what I told you here: you must see in nature the cylinder, the sphere, the cone, all put into perspective, so that every side of the object, of a plane, recedes to a central point. The parallel lines at the horizon give the extension, that is a section of nature, or, if you prefer, of the spectacle which the Omnipotent Eternal God and Father spreads before our eyes.

DA VINCI, *Leonardo*

I obey Thee, Lord, first for the love I, in all reason, owe Thee; secondly, because Thou can shorten or prolong the lives of men.

A lie is a terrible thing. Even if it spoke great things about God it would take away from God's grace.

You think that the body is a wonderful work. In reality this is nothing compared to the soul that inhabits in that structure... It is the work of God.

The works of God are appreciated best by other creators.

DELACROIX, *Eugène*

*Does nature promise us
that we shall love and
possess one another
elsewhere, without this
disquiet and anxiety that
accompany our happiest
moments? The woods
and the springs tell me so.*

God is within us: it is that inner presence which makes us admire the beautiful, which rejoices us when we have done right and consoles us for not sharing in the happiness of the wicked. It is that, beyond a doubt, which constitutes the inspiration of men of genius and which warms them at the spectacle of their own productions. There are men of virtue and men of genius; both are favoured of God.

DÜRER, *Albrecht*

And if here below thou wert like thy master Christ and sufferedst infamy at the hands of the liars of this time, and didst die a little sooner, then wouldst thou the sooner pass from death unto life and be glorified in Christ. For if thou drinkest of the cup which He drank of, with Him shalt thou reign and judge with justice those who have dealt righteously.

Oh highest heavenly Father, pour into our hearts, through Thy son, Jesus Christ, such a light, that by it we may know what messenger we are bound to obey, so that with good conscience we may lay aside the burdens of others and serve Thee, eternal, heavenly Father with happy and joyful hearts.

INGRES, *Jean Auguste Dominique*

*If God allows me and gives
me grace I will increase the
feeble contingent of my works
until the great departure.
May God make them a little
deserving for posterity.*

May God preserve us.

Have religion in your art. Do not believe that you can produce anything of worth…without the elevation of the soul. To see anything
beautiful you must see only the sublime. Do not look to the right, to
the left, or below. Look only to heaven, and don't look down toward
the earth like pigs who seek in the mud.

RENOIR, *Pierre Auguste*

I believe, therefore, without seeking to understand. I don't wish to give any name to God, to statues or to paintings. For He is above everything that is known. Everything that is made for this purpose is, in my humble opinion, a fraud.

I believe that I am nearer to God by being humble before this splendour (Nature); by accepting the role I have been given to play in life; by honouring this majesty without self interests, and, above all, without asking for anything being confident that he who has created everything has forgotten nothing.

RUBENS, *Peter Paul*

I pray to God to employ us more successfully in the future, in this and other occasions.

I CAN FINISH THE WHOLE BY THE END OF NEXT JANUARY, (GOD GRANTING ME LIFE AND BREATH).

I call the Lord to witness that I have treated him like a brother.

It rests upon the Lord God to give me life and health to bring the work to a good conclusion.

I KNOW OF NOTHING FURTHER I CAN DO, AND TRUST MY OWN GOOD CONSCIENCE AND GOD'S WILL.

I pray also that God will grant you, as well as our beloved, every sort of blessing.

Great
MUSICIANS

God ordains all for the best.

—Wolfgang Amadeus Mozart

BACH, *Johann Sebastian*

God, who sees all things.

God prescribes, carves out, calculates and arranges everything for us, and thus explains His will how He wants to be respected by us; therefore, in matters of religion we should presume and do nothing without His revealed word.

GOD IS A GOD OF ORDER.

I can only bear my cross in patience and commend my undutiful boy to God's mercy, never doubting that He will hear my sorrow-stricken prayer and in His good time bring my son to understand that the path of conversion leads to Him.

To the Highest God alone be glory.

BEETHOVEN, *Ludwig van*

God is immaterial; as He is invisible. He can, therefore, have no form. But from what we are able to perceive in His works we conclude that He is eternal, almighty, omniscient, and omnipresent. The Mighty One, He alone is free from all desire or passion. There is no greater than He... His mind is self-existent. He, the Almighty, is present in every part of space. His omniscience is self-inspired, and His conception includes every other. Of His all-embracing attributes the greatest is omniscience. For there is no threefold kind of being—it is independent of everything—O God! Thou art the true, eternal, blessed, unchangeable light of all time and space. Thy wisdom apprehends thousands and still thousands of laws, and yet Thou ever actest of Thy free will, and to Thy honor. Thou wast before all that we worship. To Thee is due praise and adoration. Thou alone art the true... Thou, the best of all laws, the image of all wisdom, present throughout the whole world. Thou sustaineth all things.

GLUCK, *Christoph Willibald von*

I commend my soul to the infinite mercy of God.

I thank God that I am healthy again.

HANDEL, *George Frideric*

Ye servants of th'eternal King
His pow'r and glory sing;
And speak of all His righteous ways
With wonder and with praise.

Oh first created beam!

And Thou great word!

Let there be light!

And light was over all.

HAYDN, *Franz Joseph*

May the Almighty grant me just enough strength, before my end, to enable me to express in music the emotion which this undeserved act of spiritual grace has awakened in me.

NEVER BEFORE WAS I SO DEVOUT AS WHEN I COMPOSED "THE CREATION." I KNELT DOWN EACH DAY TO PRAY TO GOD TO GIVE ME THE STRENGTH FOR MY WORK.

The Almighty is my support.

The Emperor Franz asked him…which product of his art he preferred, The Creation or The Seasons. "The Creation," replied Haydn. "And why?" "In the creation, angels speak and tell God, but in the Seasons only Simon talks."

I thank my Creator daily for His boon.

LISZT, *Franz*

EVERYTHING IS TRANSITORY
EXCEPT THE WORD OF GOD,
WHICH IS ETERNAL—AND
THE WORD OF GOD REVEALS
ITSELF IN THE CREATION OF
GENIUS.

Yes "Jesus Christ on the cross," a yearning longing after the Cross,—this was ever my true inner calling; I have felt it in my innermost heart ever since my seventeenth year… In spite of the transgressions and errors which I have committed, and for which I feel sincere repentance and contrition, the holy light of the Cross has never entirely withdrawn from me. At times indeed the refulgence of this Divine light has overflowed my entire soul. I thank God for this, and shall die with my soul fixed upon the Cross, our redemption and our highest bliss.

MASCAGNI, *Pietro*

We Christians know that the sweet and tender man, that alone and isolated preached goodness to humanity, was Jesus; We know that Jesus belongs to the Divinity: Father, Son and Holy Spirit; but He came on earth for His Divine mission in the likeness of mortal man, and men that heard His law of love felt new sentiments in their inspired heart… He creates, divinely creates.

I have absolute faith in God.

Jesus was Divinity; this indicates that genius is a divine gift, because only Divinity can create that which does not exist. Therefore, Jesus, having come to the earth as a man, to teach man. His new law for the good of humanity, remains Divine, but can be considered a man of genius for the creation and the preaching of His law divinely human.

ART, TO BE TRULY ART, NEEDS THE DIVINE GIFT OF CREATION.

MOZART, *Wolfgang Amadeus*

Let us trust God and comfort ourselves with the thought that all is well if it be God's will, since he best knows what is requisite and necessary to our temporal and to our eternal happiness.

God, who ordains all for the best, however strange it may appear to our eyes...

No physician, nor any other man, no accident, no chance, can either give life or take it, but God alone.

Let us submit steadfastly to the Divine will, fully convinced it will be for our good, for he does all things well.

PUCCINI, *Giacomo*

SO FAR, GOD BE THANKED, I HAVE HAD MY FULL SHARE OF SUCCESS.

I was born so many years ago…and Almighty God touched me with His little finger and said: "write only for the theatre"… And I have obeyed the supreme command.

I don't say full steam ahead, but have got started again, and God grant me good going.

May it be as God decrees and the humble subscriber desires.

PURCELL, *Henry*

*It is not fit nor decent
that such as should
sing the praises of God
Almighty should be
trained or employed in
lascivious or profane
exercises.*

MY SOUL I SURRENDER UP TO ALMIGHTY
GOD, MY CREATOR, IN THE MERITS OF
JESUS CHRIST MY REDEEMER.

RACHMANINOFF, *Sergei Wassilievitch*

No prophet I, no warrior bold

No learned mantle wearing

But as I go my harp I hold

The grace of God declaring.

Blessed art Thou, O Lord, teach me Thy statutes.

STRAVINSKY, *Igor Fëdorovich*

*My artistic goal is
to make an object...
I create the object
because God makes
me create it, just as
He created me.*

The more one separates himself from the canons of the Christian church, the further one distances oneself from the truth. These canons are true for musical compositions as they are for the life of an individual.

TCHAIKOVSKY, *Peter Ilyich*

The night has been glorious!…
The moon shone brightly. The
stillness, the perfume of the
flowers, and those wondrous,
indefinable sounds that belong
to the night—ah God, how
beautiful it all is.

For some time I have been longing to find a subject…for an
opera. Should God grant me a long life, I hope to carry out
this plan.

Whenever I think calmly over all I have been through, I come to the conclusion that there is a Providence who has specially cared for me. Not only have I been saved from ruin—which seemed at one time inevitable—but things are now well with me, and I see ahead the dawn-light of happiness and success.

God give you happiness and success.

[CHRIST] WHO PRAYED FOR HIS ENEMIES, AND PROMISED THE GOOD NO EARTHLY WEALTH, BUT RATHER THE KINGDOM OF HEAVEN! WHAT TOUCHING LOVE AND COMPASSION FOR MANKIND LIES IN THESE WORDS: "COME UNTO ME, ALL YOU THAT LABOR AND ARE HEAVY LADEN"!

God's power operates constantly

Great PHILOSOPHERS

and everywhere in all things.

—Immanuel Kant

BACON, *Francis*

God has this attribute
that He is a jealous
God; and therefore
His worship and
religion will endure
no mixture nor
partner.

They that deny a God destroy man's nobility; for certainly man is of kin
to the beasts in his body; and, if he be not of kin to God by his spirit, he
is a base and ignoble creature.

It were better to have no opinion of God at all, than such an opinion as is unworthy of him: for the one is unbelief, the other is contumely; and certainly superstition is the reproach of the Deity.

IT IS TRUE, THAT A LITTLE PHILOSOPHY INCLINETH MAN'S MIND TO ATHEISM; BUT DEPTH IN PHILOSOPHY BRINGS ABOUT MAN'S MIND TO RELIGION: FOR WHILE THE MIND OF MAN LOOKETH UPON SECOND CAUSES SCATTERED, IT MAY SOMETIMES REST IN THEM, AND GO NO FURTHER; BUT WHEN IT BEHOLDETH THE CHAIN OF THEM CONFEDERATE AND LINKED TOGETHER, IT MUST NEEDS FLY TO PROVIDENCE AND DEITY.

BRUNO, *Giordano*

The Universal Intellect is
the innermost, most real and
essential faculty and the most
efficacious part of the word-
soul. It is the one and the same
thing, which fills the whole,
illumines the universe, and
directs nature in producing her
species in the right way. It plays the same role in the production of
natural things as our intellect does in the parallel production of rational
systems.

CAUSE, PRINCIPLE, ETERNAL UNITY,

ON WHICH ALL BEING, MOTION AND LIFE DEPEND:

IN LENGTH, IN BREATH, IN DEPTH YOUR POWERS EXTEND

AS FAR AS HEAVEN AND EARTH AND HELL MAY BE—

WITH SENSE, WITH REASON, AND WITH SPIRIT I'VE SEEN

THAT RECKONING, MEASURE AND ACT CAN'T COMPREHEND

THE FORCE, THE NUMBER AND MASS, WHICH, WITH NO END,

PASS ALL THAT'S LOW OR HIGH OR SET BETWEEN.

CAMPANELLA, *Tommaso*

It is up to Thee, Oh Lord,
If you have not created me in vain,
To be my saviour
That is why night and day
I supplicate Thee with tears.
When will Thou finally hear me?
I have no more words to say,
But the chains that surround me,
They laugh and ridicule me
For my vain prayers,
My dry ears and tired supplications.

He who rises to the love of the common Father
Esteemeth all men as brothers.

I believe in God,
POWER,
Wisdom,
Love,
One,
Life,
TRUTH,
Goodness,
Infinite,
First Cause,
KING OF ALL KINGS
and *Creator.*

I come to Thee, most mighty Lord,
All knowing God.
Most loving First Cause and One:
Be merciful on our ancient sin....

Think, oh man, think;
rejoice and exalt
The First High Cause.

DESCARTES, *René*

BY THE NAME OF GOD, I UNDERSTAND
A SUBSTANCE INFINITE (ETERNAL,
IMMUTABLE), INDEPENDENT, ALL
KNOWING, ALL POWERFUL AND BY
WHICH I MYSELF, AND EVERY OTHER
THING THAT EXISTS...WERE CREATED.

The idea of a complete and independent being, that is God, presents itself to my spirit with much distinction and clarity, and it is of that only that this reality is found in me.

In God we encounter an infinity of things that I cannot understand...for my limited nature cannot comprehend the nature of the Infinite.

I have concluded the evident existence of God, and that my existence depends entirely on God in all the moments of my life, that I do not think that the human spirit may know anything with greater evidence and certitude.

It is quite evident that He [God] cannot deceive, because the natural light teaches us that deceit depends necessarily from a fault.

IT IS SUFFICIENT FOR US WHO ARE FAITHFUL TO BELIEVE BY FAITH THAT THERE IS A GOD.

It is absolutely true that we must believe in God, because it is also taught by the Holy Scriptures. On the other hand, we must believe in the Sacred Scriptures because they come from God. This we believe because of faith, being a gift from God… He who gives the grace to believe in other things can also give us faith to believe that He exists.

I conceive of God as infinite in such a high degree that nothing may be added to the perfection He possesses.

FICHTE, *Johann Gottlieb*

Nothing exists
outside of God...
and this knowing
is the divine
existence itself...
God not only is
inwardly and concealed
within Himself, but He
also exists and expresses Himself.

For freedom is always the last thing that we are willing to give up; and, if we cannot save it for ourselves, we try at least to find a refuge for it in God.

MY SCHEMING SPIRIT HAS FOUND REST, AND I THANK PROVIDENCE THAT, SHORTLY BEFORE ALL MY HOPES WERE FRUSTRATED, I WAS PLACED IN A POSITION WHICH ENABLED ME TO BEAR WITH CHEERFULNESS THE DISAPPOINTMENT.

God is pure being. But his being in itself is not, so to speak, compression; it is, throughout, agility, transparency, light… It is being, only for the finite reason, but not in itself.

FICHTE (cont.)

God Himself... the inner essence of the Absolute, which is distinguished from its outer existence only for our fortitude.

One thinks of God as conceiving the moral life of man as the sole purpose for the sake of which He has manifested Himself and has called everything else except this moral life into existence...not as if it were really so (as if God thought in the way in which finite beings think, and as if for Him existence were something different from the idea of existence), but simply because we are not able to conceive the relation in any other way. And in this absolutely necessary mode of representation, human life becomes, as it ought to be, the Idea, God's chief thought in producing the world, the purpose and the plan, whose carrying out God decreed when He decreed the world.

WHAT IS OUTSIDE GOD DISSOLVES
INTO MERE PERCEPTION, IMAGE,
KNOWING...AND IN IT THERE IS
NOT THE SLIGHTEST TRACE OR
GLEAM OF TRUE FORMAL BEING,
WHICH REMAINS WHOLLY IN GOD.

In the beginning wholly independent of all possibility of
the opposite, independent of all arbitrariness, all chance,
and thus of all time, grounded in the inner necessity of
the divine essence itself, was the form. And the form
was with God...and the form itself was God: thus God
came forth in it just as He is in Himself.

HEGEL, *Georg Wilhelm Friedrich*

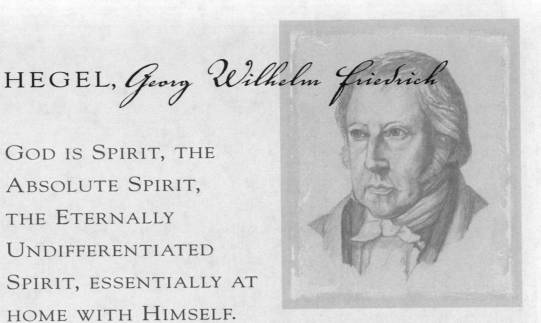

GOD IS SPIRIT, THE ABSOLUTE SPIRIT, THE ETERNALLY UNDIFFERENTIATED SPIRIT, ESSENTIALLY AT HOME WITH HIMSELF.

God in His universality…in which there is no limitation, no finiteness, no particularity, is the absolute self-subsisting being and the only self-subsisting being; and what subsists has its roots, its subsistence, in this one alone.

God is the One absolutely self-sufficient Being.

ALL IS GOD.

To think of God means to rise above what is sensuous, external and individual. It means to rise up to what is pure, to that which is in unity with itself; it is a going forth above and beyond the sensuous, beyond what belongs to the sphere of the senses into the pure regions of the universal. And this region is thought.

God is the beginning of all things, and the end of all things. As all things precede from this point, so all return back.

IN GOD THERE IS NO EVIL.

God is good, and good alone.

JAMES, *William*

I do not know what the
sweat and blood and
tragedy of this life may
mean if they mean
anything short of this.
If this life be not a real
fight, in which something is
eternally gained for the
universe by success, it is
no better than a game of
private theatricals from
which one may withdraw at will. But it feels like a real fight—as if there
were something really wild in the universe which we, with all our ideali-
ties and faithfulnesses, are needed to redeem; and first of all to redeem
our own hearts from atheisms and fears.

KANT, *Immanuel*

THE SUM TOTAL OF ALL
POSSIBLE KNOWLEDGE OF
GOD IS NOT POSSIBLE FOR
A HUMAN BEING, NOT
EVEN THROUGH A TRUE
REVELATION. BUT IT IS
ONE OF THE WORTHIEST
INQUIRIES TO SEE HOW FAR
OUR REASON CAN GO IN
THE KNOWLEDGE OF GOD.

God's omnipresence is not local, but virtual. That is, God's power operates constantly and everywhere in all things.

God has no need of experience at all. He knows everything a priori, because he himself created everything he cares for; and everything is possible only through him. Hence God formulated the laws governing the world in light of a true acquaintance with every single event which would be given in the course of it. And in the establishment of the world's course he certainly had the greatest possible perfection in view, because God himself is the all wise and is All in all.

KANT *(cont.)*

God is the only ruler of the world. He governs as a monarch, but not as a despot; for he wills to have his commands observed out of love, and not out of servile fear. Like a father, he orders what is good for us, and does not command out of mere arbitrariness, like a tyrant. God even demands of us that we reflect on the reason for his commandments, and he insists on our observing them because he wants first to make us worthy of happiness and then participate in it. God's will is benevolence, and his purpose is what is best. If God commands something for which we cannot see the reason, then this is because of the limitation of our knowledge, and not because of the nature of the commandment itself. God carries out His rulership of the world *alone*. For he surveys everything with one glance. And certainly he may often use wholly incomprehensible means to carry out his benevolent aims.

God created the world for his honor's sake because it is only through the obedience to his holy laws that God can be honored. For what does it mean to honor God? What, if not to serve him? But how can he be served? Certainly not by trying to entice his favor by rendering him all sorts of praise. For such praise is at best only a means for preparing our hearts to a good disposition. Instead, the service of God consists simply and solely in following his will and observing his holy laws and commands.

MORALITY LEADS INFALLIBLY TO RELIGION, BY WHICH IT EXPANDS TO THE IDEA OF A MORAL, ALL-POWERFUL LEGISLATOR WHO IS EXTERNAL TO MAN WHO HAS IN HIS WILL THE FINAL END (OF THE CREATION OF THE WORLD), THAT, AT THE SAME TIME, MAY AND HAS TO BE THE FINAL END OF MAN.

The true (moral) worship of God, that believers owe him, being subjects of his kingdom, as well as citizens of the same, invisible, I mean a worship from the heart, (in spirit and in truth) and it can consist in the intention to observe all the true duties as the commandments of God and not in acts destined exclusively to God.

KIERKEGAARD, *Sören*

All other religions are indirect. Their founder sets himself aside and introduces another in his place… Christianity only is a direct expression (I am the truth).

What is special about my relationship with God is the fact that it is a relationship based on reflection.

I HAVE A CHILD-FATHER RELATIONSHIP WITH PROVIDENCE.

God is infinitely distant from selfishness. He is absolute selflessness.

Christianity teaches categorically that enemies must be loved, since even a pagan loves his friends. Love for one's enemies is only possible by God, because we love God... When we love our enemies we show the evidence that we fear and love God, only thus he can be loved.

If I am infinitely nothing. Then, it is sure that God loves me. Because, before God, I am less than nothing, it is, therefore, more sure that God loves me.

I AM SEEING EVERMORE CLEARLY THAT ALL WHO GOD HAS LOVED... ALL HAD TO SUFFER IN THE WORLD... THIS IS THE CHRISTIAN DOCTRINE: BEING LOVED OF GOD MEANS LOVING GOD AND SUFFERING.

KIERKEGAARD *(cont.)*

He who is totally weak, it is in him that God is strong.

WHEN CHRIST CRIED "MY GOD, MY GOD, WHY HAVE YOU FORSAKEN ME?" IT WAS A TERRIBLE MOMENT FOR CHRIST. BUT, I BELIEVE, THAT IT WAS MORE TERRIBLE FOR GOD TO HEAR HIS CRY. IMMUTABLE BEING, LOVE BEING, WHAT INFINITE SADNESS, DEEP, INCOMPREHENSIBLE.

God is infinite love, given that He does not land abruptly on a man. No, He seizes gently. It's a slow operation; an education.

For as long as a man does not understand how great a sinner he is, he cannot love God…he cannot understand what a great sinner he is.

WORLDLY WISDOM TEACHES THAT LOVE IS THE RELATIONSHIP BETWEEN MAN AND MAN. CHRISTIANITY TEACHES THAT LOVE IS THE RELATIONSHIP BETWEEN MAN AND GOD.

He who sees his brother suffer in need and does not help him excludes God from his heart.

In loving God you become one with God.

LEIBNIZ, *Gottfried Wilhelm von*

For what greater master can we find than God, the author of the universe? And what more beautiful hymn can we sing to Him than one in which the witness of things themselves expresses His praise? But the more one can give reasons for His love, the more one loves God… Nor should we think that anything is badly arranged in the universe or that God neglects those who honor Him.

With absolute certainty, there is nothing more true than this [God's existence] and that we have the idea of God, and that the Being that is supremely perfect is possible, more than He is necessary.

GOD...HAS NO NEED FOR MATTER; HE NOT ONLY ARRANGES IT, HE ALSO MAKES IT... WHETHER HE SHAPES IT OR BREAKS IT HE IS WISE AND HE DOES WHAT HE WANTS, AND WHAT HE WANTS IS ALWAYS GOOD. HE HAS THE RIGHT TO MAKE IT; HE SHOWS AND EXERCISES HIS DOMINION; HE IS ALL, AND MATTER IS NOTHING FOR HIM.

Power and knowledge are perfections and insofar as they belong to God, have no limits. Hence it follows that God, who possesses supreme and infinite wisdom, acts in the most perfect way and does this not only in a metaphysical but also in a moral sense.

If the smallest of evils that occur in the world would not occur, it would not be the world, that, all considered and pondered, has appeared best to the Creator that has chosen it. Certainly, we can imagine possible worlds that have no sin and no hardship...but those worlds would be much less inferior to our own.

LEIBNIZ *(cont.)*

Let's consider God as a being who is supremely perfect, that is a Being in Whom perfection admits no limits; It will appear, then, clearly, that it is not less repugnant to conceive of a God (That is a God who is supremely perfect), who does not exist, (That is who is missing some perfection), than to conceive of a mountain that has no valley. In virtue of only this consideration, and without recourse to any developed proof, we recognize that God exists.

I HAVE ALWAYS BEEN IN FAVOR, AND I STILL AM, OF THE INNATE IDEA OF GOD.

No sleep may last forever; but it will last less, or almost not at all, for reasonable souls, perpetually destined to preserve the personality and the memory, that was given to them, in the City of God.

When we separate things that are tied together, the parts from the whole, humanity from the universe, the attributes of God one from the other, power from wisdom; it is permissible to say that God can make virtue be in the world without it mixing with vice… But, since He has permitted vice, then the order of the universe, found to be preferable to any other plan, has demanded it.

God, who is the inventor and the architect regarding the workings of nature, becomes King and Father regarding the substances that have intelligence, and whose soul is a spirit formed in His image. Regarding the spirits, of whom they are citizens, and the most perfect monarchy they can invent, where there is no sin that will not attract some penalty, nor a good action without recompense; where all tends finally to the glory of the Monarch, and the happiness of the subjects, for the most beautiful union of justice and goodness that can be desired.

I find God and His glory everywhere.

Wise and virtuous people strive to do all that is according to the Divine will presently or past and, therefore, they are satisfied with what God does effectively, by His secret will…recognizing that, if we had enough understanding of the order of the universe, we would find that it surpasses the desire of all the wise, and that it is impossible to make it better than what it is, not only regarding everything in general, but even we in particular, if we are bonded to the author of all, not only as the architect and the dynamic cause of our being, but also as to our Lord and to the final cause, that has to constitute the end of our will, and that only can be the cause of our happiness.

MILL, *John Stuart*

I think it must be allowed that, in the present state of our knowledge, the adaptations in nature afford a large balance of probability in favour of creation by intelligence.

AMONG THE FACTS OF THE UNIVERSE TO BE ACCOUNTED FOR, IT MAY BE SAID, IS MIND; AND IT IS SELF EVIDENT THAT NOTHING CAN HAVE PRODUCED MIND BUT MIND.

In voluntary action alone we see a commencement, an origination of motion; since all other causes appear incapable of this origination experience is in favour of the conclusion that all the motion in existence owed this beginning to this one cause, voluntary agency, if not that of man, then of a more powerful being.

PASCAL, *Blaise*

Let man reverting to himself, consider what he is compared with all that exists. Let him behold himself a wanderer in this secluded province of nature, and by what he can see from the little dungeon in which he finds himself lodged, (I mean the visible universe), let him learn to make a right estimate of the earth, its kingdoms, its cities and himself.

All things have sprung from nothing and are borne forward to infinity. Who can follow out such an astonishing career? The Author of these wonders, and He alone, can comprehend them.

Every thing in the world shows either the unhappy condition of man, or the mercy of God; either the weakness of man without God, or the power of man assisted by God. The whole universe bears witness to the corruption or the redemption of man. Every thing betokens His grandeur or His degradation. The withdrawment of God is seen among the Pagan; the protection of God is seen among the Jews.

Instead of complaining that God is so concealed, it is the duty of men to bless Him, that He has so far revealed Himself, and also, that He has not discovered Himself to the worldly wise, or to the proud, who are unworthy to know so holy a God.

The stoics said, retire into yourselves, there you will find repose: but this was not true;—others said, Go out of yourselves and seek for happiness in amusement: and this, too, was wrong. There are diseases ready to destroy these delusions: happiness can be found neither in ourselves nor in external things, but in God and in ourselves as united to Him.

IT IS INVARIABLY TRUE, THAT HE CONCEALS HIMSELF FROM THOSE WHO TEMPT HIM, AND MANIFESTS HIMSELF TO THOSE WHO SEEK HIM.

I perceive it is possible I might not have existed, for my essence consists in the thinking principle; therefore I, this thinking being, should never have existed, had my mother been killed before I was animated:—then I am not a necessary being. Nor am I eternal or infinite, but I see plainly, that there is in nature, a necessary, eternal, and infinite Being.

PICO DELLA MIRANDOLA, *Giovanni*

We conceive God as the university of all act, the plenitude of existence.

GOD IS MOST TRUE.

God is the fullest being, individual unity, most solid truth, most blessed good.

God is infinite perfections of every sort.

GOD IS

BEING ITSELF,

THE ONE ITSELF,

THE GOOD ITSELF,

THE, LIKEWISE,

TRUTH ITSELF.

Now the highest Father, God the master-builder, had, by the laws of His secret wisdom, fabricated this house, this world which we see, a very superb temple of divinity. He had adorned the super-celestial region with minds. He had animated the super-celestial globes with eternal souls; He had filled with a diverse throng of animals the cast-off and residual parts of the lower world. But, with the work finished, the Artisan desired that there be someone to reckon up the reason of such a big work, to love its beauty, and to wonder at its greatness.

ROUSSEAU, *Jean Jacques*

If God exists,
He is perfect;
if He is perfect
He is wise,
powerful and just;
if He is wise and powerful,
everything is for the best.

(The Bible) is in my opinion the most
sublime of all books; when all others
will bore me, I will always go back to it
with new pleasure; and when all
human consolations will be lacking,
never have I vainly turned to its own.

I WILL NEVER KNOW HIM
BY HIS BEING. I CAN
ONLY, THEREFORE, STUDY
HIM BY HIS ATTRIBUTES.

…forgive me, great man my fervour which is perhaps indiscreet…but the question at issue is the cause of Providence, which only is my solace… I have suffered too much in my life not to look forward to another. Not all the subtleties of metaphysics can shake for one moment my belief in a beneficent Providence. I sense the existence of Providence, I believe in it, I insist on it, I hope for it, I shall defend it to my last breath…

An intelligent being, is the active principle of all things. One must have renounced common sense to doubt it, and it is a waste of time to try to prove such self evident truth.

NO, GOD OF MY SOUL, I WILL NEVER BLAME YOU FOR HAVING MADE HIM [MAN] IN YOUR IMAGE, SO AS TO BE FREE, GOOD AND HAPPY AS YOU ARE.

The blackboard of nature offers me harmony and proportion, that of human beings offers me confusion and disorder. Harmony reigns among the elements while men are in chaos! Animals are happy, their king only is miserable!

Worship the Eternal Being…and by so doing in one breath you will destroy the ghosts of reason, that are nothing but a vain manifestation that runs as a shadow before the immutable truth. Nothing exists but by Him who is…it is His unchangeable substance that is the true model of perfections of which we have an image within ourselves.

SPINOZA, *Benedict de*

*We cannot be more
certain of the
existence of anything,
than the existence of
a being absolutely
infinite or perfect—
that is, of God.*

WITHOUT GOD NOTHING CAN BE CONCEIVED.

God and His attributes are unchangeable.

BESIDES GOD NO SUBSTANCE IS GRANTED OR CAN BE CONCEIVED.

GOD AND HIS ATTRIBUTES ARE ETERNAL.

Things have been brought into being by God in the highest perfection, inasmuch as they have necessarily followed from a most perfect nature.

Wherefore the omnipotence of God has been displayed from all eternity, and will for all eternity remain in the same activity.

VOLTAIRE

All nature cries to us that He exists, that there is a Supreme Intelligence, a power immense, an order admirable, and all teaches us our dependence.

WHAT IS TRUE RELIGION? LOVE GOD AND YOUR NEIGHBOR AS YOURSELF.

We want a religion that is simple, wise, grand, worthy of God and made for us; in one word we want to serve God and men.

Let's worship this great Being… It is He who from all eternity arranged matter in the immensity of space.

[God] is the supreme being. He is unique, infinite, eternal, creator of the world.

If God did not exist, everything would be allowed.

PRAYING MEANS SUBMITTING.

I die, adoring God, loving friends, not hating my enemies and detesting superstitions.

Tonight I was in a meditative mood. I was absorbed in the contemplation of nature; I admired the immensity, the movements, the harmony of those infinite globes…I admired still more the intelligence which directs these vast forces. I said to myself: "One must be blind not to be dazzled by this spectacle; one must be stupid not to recognize the author of it; one must be mad not to worship Him."

CHRIST CONSOLES IN SECRET THE HEARTS HE ENLIGHTENS. IN THE GREATEST OF TRIALS, HE OFFERS THEM SUPPORT.

[God is] supreme logic, a distant home.

If God did not exist, it would be necessary to invent Him.

WEIL, *Simone*

One must feel the reality and the presence of God in all external objects without exception, as surely that the hand feels the consistency of the paper through nib and the pen.

It is in affliction itself that the splendor of God's mercy shines, from its very depths, in the heart of its inconsolable bitterness.

The cross is enough for me.

I was brought up by my parents and my brother in a complete agnosticism, and I never made the slightest effort to depart from it; I never had the slightest desire to do so… In spite of that, ever since my birth…not one of my faults, not one of my imperfections really had the excuse of ignorance. I shall have to answer for everything in that day when the Lamb shall come in anger.

God has created by love for love. He has created all the forms of love.

CHRIST… IS TRUTH ITSELF.

We should give God the strict minimum of place in our lives, that which it is absolutely impossible for us to refuse Him—and earnestly desire that one day, and as soon as possible, that strict minimum may become all.

WEIL *(cont.)*

Every existing thing is equally upheld in its existence by God's creative love. The friends of God should love Him to the point of merging their love into His with regard to all things here below.

I DO NOT NEED ANY HOPE OR ANY PROMISE TO KNOW THAT GOD IS RICH IN MERCY. I KNOW THE WEALTH OF HIS WITH THE CERTAINTY OF EXPERIENCE; I HAVE TOUCHED IT.

I am as totally sure of God's existence as I am sure that my love is not an illusion.

GOD IS ABSOLUTE GOODNESS.

Christ descended and took me...this meeting took place without the intermediary action of any human being.

If we really love God, we necessarily think of Him as being, amongst other things, the soul of the world; for love is always connected with a body, and God has no other body which is offered to our senses except the universe itself. Then each occurrence, whatever it may be, is like a touch on the part of God; each even, each thing that takes place, whether it be fortunate, unfortunate or unimportant from our particular point of view, is a caress of God's.

WITTGENSTEIN, *Ludwig*

Certainly it is
correct to say;
conscience is the
voice of God.

How things stand is God. God is how things stand.

The meaning of life,
(i.e., the meaning of the
world), we can call God.
And connect with this
the comparison of God
to a father.

What we are dependent on we call God.

THE GOOD IS WHAT GOD ORDERS.

*To pray is to think about the meaning of life...
To believe in a God means to see the facts of the
world are not the end of the matter. To believe in
God means to see that life has a meaning.*

I want to know how God created the world. I want to know

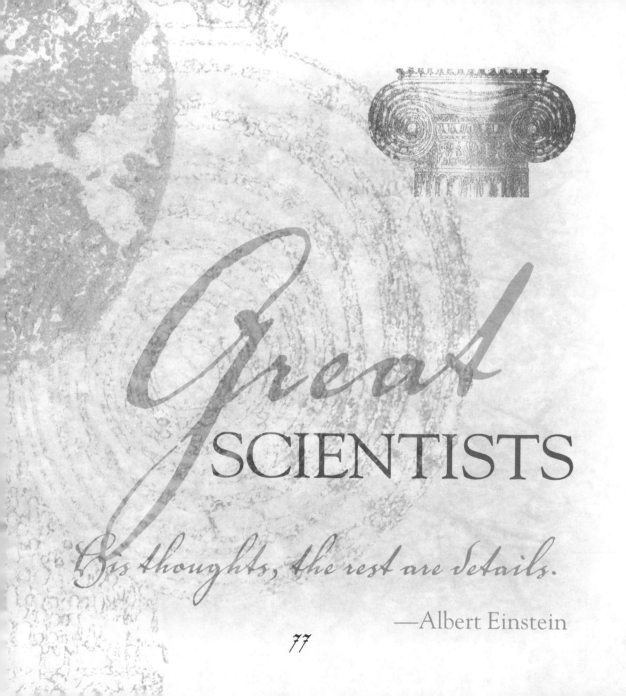

Great SCIENTISTS

His thoughts, the rest are details.

—Albert Einstein

BRAHE, *Tycho*

GOD...FROM WHOM
WE ACKNOWLEDGE
ALL THINGS TO BE
RECEIVED.

It is impossible to set forth a certain time for the consummation of the world, which only dependeth upon the good will and pleasure of God, and is not revealed to angels, and therefore cannot be known by any human prescience.

God who ruleth the heavens shall rule all things on earth.

COPERNICUS, *Nicolaus*

God, without whom we can do nothing.

For who, after applying himself to things which he sees established in the best order and directed by divine ruling, would not through contemplation and them and through a certain habituation be awakened to that which is best and would not admire the Artificer of all things, in Whom is all happiness and every good? For the divine psalmist surely did not say gratuitously that he took pleasure in the workings of God and rejoiced in the works of His hands, unless by means of those things as by some sort of vehicle we are transported to the contemplation of the highest good.

EINSTEIN, *Albert*

I defend the
Good God
against the idea
of a continuous
game of dice.

YOU BELIEVE IN GOD PLAYING DICE, AND I IN
PERFECT LAWS IN THE WORLD OF THINGS
EXISTING AS REAL OBJECTS, WHICH I TRY TO
GRASP IN A WILDLY SPECULATIVE WAY.

I'm not much with people, and I'm not a family man. I want my peace. I want to know how God created this world. I am not interested in this or that phenomenon in the spectrum of this or that element. I want to know His thoughts, the rest are details.

I believe in... God, who reveals Himself in the harmony of all being.

The scientist's religious feeling takes the form of a rapturous amazement at the harmony of natural law, which reveals an intelligence of such superiority that, compared with it, all the systematic thinking and acting of human beings is an utterly insignificant reflection.

FARADAY, *Michael*

And though the thought of death brings the thought of judgment, which is far above all the trouble that arises from the breaking of mere earthly ties, it also brings to the Christian the thought of Him who died, was judged and who rose again for the justification of those who believe in Him.

Though we may well fear for ourselves and our faith, much more may we trust in Him who is faithful; and though we have the treasures in earthen vessels, and so are surrounded by the infirmities of the flesh with all the accompanying hesitation—temptations and the attacks of the Adversary—yet it is that the excellency of the power of God may be with us.

The Christian…is taught of God (by His Word and the Holy Spirit) to trust in the promise of salvation through the work of Jesus Christ. He finds his guide in the Word of God, and commits the keeping of his soul into the hands of God. He looks for no assurance beyond what the Word can give him, and if his mind is troubled by the cares and fears which may assail him, he can go nowhere but in his prayer to the throne of grace and to the Scripture.

I bow before Him who is Lord of all, and hope to be kept waiting patiently for His time and mode of releasing me according to His Divine Word, and the great and precious promises whereby His people are made partakers of the Divine nature.

I AM CONTENT TO BEAR THE REPROACH; YET, EVEN IN EARTHLY MATTERS, I BELIEVE THAT THE INVISIBLE THINGS OF HIM FROM THE CREATION OF THE WORLDS ARE CLEARLY SEEN, BEING UNDERSTOOD BY THE THINGS WHICH ARE MADE, EVEN HIS ETERNAL POWER AND GODHEAD.

GALILEI, *Galileo*

*May it be our lot,
by the grace of the
true Son, pure and
immaculate, to learn
from Him, with all
other truths, that
which we are now
seeking.*

ONE MUST NOT DOUBT THE POSSIBILITY THAT THE
DIVINE GOODNESS AT TIMES MAY CHOOSE TO INSPIRE A
RAY OF HIS IMMENSE KNOWLEDGE IN LOW AND HIGH
INTELLECTS WHEN THEY ARE ADORNED WITH SINCERE
AND HOLY ZEAL.

When I reflect on so many profoundly marvellous things that persons have grasped, sought, and done I recognize even more clearly that human intelligence is a work of God, and one of the most excellent.

To the Lord; whom I worship and thank;

That governs the heavens with His eyelid

To Him I return tired, but full of living.

I trust the infinite goodness of God may direct toward the purity of my mind a small amount of His grace that I may understand the meaning of His words.

God could have made birds with bones of massive gold, with veins full of molten silver, with flesh heavier than lead and with tiny wings… He could have made fish heavier than lead, and thus twelve times heavier than water, but He has wished to make the former of bone, flesh, and feathers that are light enough, and the latter as heavier than water, to teach us that He rejoices in simplicity and facility.

HARVEY, *William*

We acknowledge God, the Supreme and Omnipotent Creator, to be present in the production of all animals… All things are indeed contrived and ordered with singular providence, divine wisdom, and most admirable and incomprehensible skill. And to none can these attributes be referred save to the Almighty…

The Omnipotent Maker of all things…upon Whom all animals and their births depend: and at Whose beck, or mandate, all things are created and begotten.

The examination of the bodies of animals [manifests] a kind of…reflection of the omnipotent Creator Himself.

KEPLER, *Johann*

Geometry…coeternal with God…
and reflecting in the Divine mind has
supplied God with the examples…
for the furnishing of the world so that
it became the best and most beautiful,
and (even) also the most similar to
the Creator.

But we Christians…know that the eternal and uncreated Logos who was with God and
who is contained by no abode…has occupied the heavens as His royal abode.

Great is our Lord and great is His strength and there is no number to His wisdom.
Praise Him heavens, praise Him sun, moon, planets, whatever sense you may use to
perceive, whatever tongue to express our Creator. Praise Him heavenly harmonies,
praise Him you witnesses of the (now) detected harmonies. Praise also you, my soul,
your Lord the Creator as long as I shall be. For from Him and through Him, and in
Him is all… To Him be praise, honour and glory into all eternity. Amen.

NEWTON, *Sir Isaac*

THE SUPREME GOD EXISTS

NECESSARILY, AND BY THE

SAME NECESSITY HE EXISTS

ALWAYS AND EVERYWHERE.

From His true dominion it follows that the true God is a living, intelligent and powerful being; and from His other perfections, that He is supreme, or most perfect. He is eternal and infinite, omnipotent and omniscient; that is, His duration reaches from eternity to eternity; His presence from infinity to infinity; He governs all things, and knows all things that are or can be done.

As a blind man has no idea of colours, so have we no idea of the manner by which the all-wise God perceives and understands all things. He is utterly void of all body and bodily figure, and can, therefore neither be seen or heard or touched; nor ought He to be worshipped under the representation of any corporeal thing. We have ideas of His attributes but what the real substance of anything is we know not. In bodies we see only their figures and colours, we hear only the sound, we touch only their outward surfaces, we smell only the smells and taste the savours, but their inward substances are not to be known either by our senses or by any reflex act of our minds; much less, then, have we any idea of the substance of God. We know Him only by His most wise and excellent con-trivances of things and final causes; we admire Him for His perfections, but we reverence and adore Him on account of His dominion, for we adore Him as His servants.

HE ENDURETH FOREVER, AND IS EVERYWHERE PRESENT; AND BY EXISTING ALWAYS AND EVERYWHERE, HE CONSTITUTES DURATION AND SPACE ...IN HIM ARE ALL THINGS CONTAINED AND MOVED.

PASTEUR, *Louis*

In good philosophy, the word cause ought to be reserved to the single divine impulse that has formed the universe.

THE ATMOSPHERE IN WHICH WE LIVE SWARMS WITH THE GERMS OF THOSE MICROSCOPIC CREATURES, WHICH ARE ALWAYS READY TO MULTIPLY IN DEAD MATTER WHEREVER IT PRESENTS ITSELF, AND THUS TO FULFILL THE MISSION OF DESTRUCTION WHICH IS CORRELATIVE TO THEIR LIFE. AND IF GOD HAD NOT SO ARRANGED THINGS THAT, UNDER NORMAL CONDITIONS OF LIFE AND HEALTH, THE LAWS GOVERNING THE CHANGES IN TISSUES AND FLUIDS OF ANIMALS' BODIES DID NOT IMPEDE THE PROLIFERATION OF THESE MICROSCOPIC CREATURES, WE SHOULD ALWAYS BE VULNERABLE TO THEIR INROADS.

All writing

Great
WRITERS
comes from the grace of God.

—Ralph Waldo Emerson

ALIGHIERI, *Dante*

We should know, in this regard, that God and nature create nothing in vain, and that whatever is created serves some purpose.

MANKIND IS BEST WHEN IT FOLLOWS THE FOOTSTEPS OF HEAVEN AS FAR AS ITS NATURE PERMITS.

Christ...is the door of our eternal dwelling.

I believe in one God sole and eternal, who
Moves the whole universe
With love and with desire;
And for such belief I have proofs
Physical and metaphysical, and
Also the truth that rains
From Moses, the Prophets and the Psalms.

GOD ALONE ELEVATES. HE ALONE ESTABLISHES GOVERNMENTS.

The glory of Him who moves all
Penetrates the universe, and is resplendent
In one part more and less in another.

Whatever in human society God really wills must be regarded as truly and genuinely right.

BRONTË, *Emily*

NO COWARD SOUL IS MINE

No coward soul is mine,
No trembler in the world's storm-troubled sphere:
I see Heaven's glory shine,
And faith shines equal, arming me from fear.

O God within my breast,
Almighty, ever-present Deity!
Life, that in me has rest,
As I, undying life, have power in Thee!

Vain are the thousand creeds
That move man's hearts: unutterably vain;
Worthless as withered weeds,
Or idlest froth amid the boundless main,

To waken doubt in one
Holding so fast by Thy infinity,
So surely anchored on
The steadfast rock of immortality.

With wide-embracing love
Thy Spirit animates eternal years,
Pervades and broods above,
Changes, sustains, dissolves, creates, and rears.

Though earth and moon were gone,
And suns and universes ceased to be,
And Thou wert left alone,
Every existence would exist in Thee.

There is not room for Death,
Nor atom that His might could render void:
Thou — THOU art Being and Breath,
And what THOU art may never be destroyed.

THE WORLD IS NOT
NECESSARY TO
GOD AS GOD IS TO
THE WORLD. BUT,
IT IS THE EXPRES-
SION OF HIS MIND,
AND THE FIELD IN
WHICH HIS
THOUGHTS AND
PURPOSES ARE
BEING ACTUALIZED.
WHATEVER WE
CAN LEARN ABOUT
NATURE TEACHES
US ABOUT GOD.

BROWNING, *Elizabeth Barrett*

So oft the doing of God's will
Our foolish heart undoeth!
And yet what idle dream breaks ill,
Which morning-light subdueth?
And who would murmur and misdoubt,
When God's great sunrise find him out?

God hath transfixed us,—we, so moved before,
Attain to a calm. Ay, shouldering weights of pain,
We anchor in deep waters, safe from shore,
And hear submissive o'er the stormy main
God's chartered judgements walk for evermore.

GOD IS THE PERFECT POET.

God keeps His holy mysteries
Just on the outside of man's dream.

THE MEASURE

Hymn IV

I

GOD THE CREATOR, WITH A PULSELESS HAND
OF UNORIGINATED POWER, HATH WEIGHED
THE DUST OF EARTH AND TEARS OF MAN IN ONE
MEASURE, AND BY ONE WEIGHT:
SO SAITH HIS HOLY BOOK.

II

SHALL WE, THEN, WHO HAVE ISSUED FROM THE DUST
AND THERE RETURN,—SHALL WE, WHO TOIL FOR DUST,
AND WRAP OUR WINNINGS IN THIS DUSTY LIFE,
SAY "NO MORE TEARS, LORD GOD!
THE MEASURE RUNNETH O'ER"?

III

OH, HOLDER OF THE BALANCE, LAUGHEST THOU?
NAY, LORD! BE GENTLER TO OUR FOOLISHNESS,
FOR HIS SAKE WHO ASSUMED OUR DUST AND TURNS
ON THEE PATHETIC EYES
STILL MOISTENED WITH OUR TEARS.

IV

AND TEACH US, O OUR FATHER, WHILE WE WEEP,
TO LOOK IN PATIENCE UPON THE EARTH AND LEARN—
WAITING, IN THE MEEK GESTURE, TILL AT LAST
THESE TEARFUL EYES BE FILLED
WITH THE DRY DUST OF DEATH.

BROWNING, *Robert*

FROM "CHRISTMAS-EVE"

V

From the heart beneath, as if, God speeding me,
I entered His church door, nature leading me
—In youth I looked to these very skies,
and probing their immensities,
I found God there, His visible power;

....

My soul brought all to a single test
That He the Eternal First and Last,
Who, in His power, had so surpassed
All man conceives of what is might,
Whose wisdom, too, showed infinite,
Would prove as infinitely good;

....
And I shall behold Thee, face to face,
O God, and in Thy light retrace
How in all I loved Thee, still wast Thou!
Whom pressing to, then, as I fain would now,
I shall find as able to satiate
The love, Thy gift, as my spirit's wonder
Thou art able to quicken and sublimate,
With this sky of Thine, that I now walk under,
And glory in Thee for, as I gaze
Thus, thus! Oh, let men keep their ways
Of seeking Thee in a narrow shrine—
Be this my way! And this mine!

VII
Thou art the love of God—above
His power, didst hear me place His love,
And that was leaving the world for Thee.
Therefore Thou must not turn from me
As I had chosen the other part!
Folly and pride o'ercame my heart.
Our best is bad, nor bear Thy test;
Still, it should be our very best.
I thought it best that Thou, the spirit,
Be worshiped in spirit and in truth,
And in beauty, as even we require it—

BROWNING, *Robert (cont.)*

Not in the forms burlesque, uncouth,
I left but now, as scarcely fitted
For Thee: I knew not what I pitied.
But, all I felt there, right or wrong,
What is it to Thee, who curest sinning?
Am I not weak as Thou art strong?
I have looked to Thee from the beginning,
Straight up to Thee through all the world

....

Which, like an idle scroll, lay furled
To nothingness on either side:
And since the time Thou wast descried,
Spite of the weak heart, so have I
Lived ever, and so fain would die,
Living and dying, Thee before!
But if Thou leavest me—

IX

In flows heaven, with its new day
Of endless life, when He who trod,
Very man and very God,
This earth is weakness, shame and pain,
Dying the death whose signs remain
Up yonder on the accursed tree,—
Shall come again, no more to be
Of captivity the thrall,
But the one God, All in all,
King of kings, Lords of lords,
As His servant John received the words,
I died, and live for evermore!

XVI

So what is left for us, save, in growth
Of soul, to rise up, for the past both,
From the gift looking to the giver,
And from the cistern to the river,
And from the finite to infinity,
And from man's dust to God's divinity?

XVII

Supreme in Christ as we all confess,
Why need we prove would avail no jot
To make Him God, if God He were not?

BROWNING, *Robert (cont.)*

FROM "EASTER DAY"

I

How very hard it is to be

A Christian! Hard for you and me,

—Not the mere task of making real

That duty up to its ideal,

Effecting thus, complete and whole,

A purpose of the human soul—

For that is always hard to do;

But hard, I mean, for me and you

To realize it, more or less,

With even the moderate success

Which commonly repays our strife

To carry out the aims of life.

XXXI

Thou Love of God! Or let me die,

Or grant what shall seem heaven almost!

Let me not know that all is lost,

Though lost it be—leaves me not tied

To this despair, this corpse-like bride!

Let that old life seem mine—no more—

With limitation as before,

With darkness, hunger, toil, distress:

Be all the earth a wilderness!

Only let me go on, go on,

Still hoping ever and anon

To reach one eve the Better Land!

CHAUCER, *Geoffrey*

I thank the Lord Jesus Christ…[and beseech him] to send me grace to bewail my guilts and to study to the salvation of my soul, and grant me grace of true repentance…through the benign grace of Him that is King of kings and Priest over all priests, that bought us with the precious blood of His heart.

Now pray them that hearken this little treatise or read, that if there be any-thing in it that pleases them, that thereof they thank our Lord Jesus Christ, of whom proceeds all wit and all goodness. And if there be anything that displeases them, I pray them also that they charge it to my ignorance and not to my will… For our Book saith, "All that is written is written for our doctrine"—and that is mine intent. Wherefore I beseech them meekly, for the mercy of God, that they pray for me that Christ have mercy on me and forgive my guilts, and namely of my translations and compositions of wordly vanities…that Christ for His great mercy forgive me the sin.

CHEKHOV, *Anton Pavlovich*

One should believe in God; if one does not have faith, though, its place should not be taken by sound and fury but by seeking and more seeking, seeking alone, face to face with one's conscience.

PRESENT-DAY CULTURE IS BUT THE BEGINNING OF...WORK WHICH WILL PERHAPS CONTINUE FOR TENS OF THOUSANDS OF YEARS WITH THE RESULT THAT, FINALLY...MANKIND WILL PERCEIVE THE TRUTH OF THE REAL GOD, THAT IS NOT MAKE CONJECTURES...BUT PERCEIVE HIM ...AS THEY PERCEIVE THAT TWO TIMES TWO IS FOUR.

DEFOE, *Daniel*

To say it is not to be expected God should cause such a host of glorious spirits to attend on this little point, the earth, and this despicable species called man, would be but to oblige me to say: "what, may not God be supposed to do for that creature whom he loved so as to send his only begotten son to redeem?"

God…has posted an army of ministering spirits, call them angels if you will…I say posted them around this convex, this globe, the earth, to be ready at all events, to execute His orders and to do His will reserving still to Himself to send express messengers of a superior rank on extraordinary occasions. These may, without any absurdity, be supposed capable of assuming shape. Conversing with mankind, either in ordinary or extraordinary way, either by voice or sound, though in appearances and borrowed shapes, or by private notices of things, impulses, forebodings, misgivings, and other imperceptible communications to the minds of men, as God their great employer may direct.

DELEDDA, *Grazia*

I love my fellow man,
I love those who suffer,
I love my God.

I see my future clearly, and because I can see that
God loves me, I wait for my destiny with serenity.

DICKENS, *Charles*

I now most solemnly impress upon you the truth and beauty of the Christian religion, as it came from Christ Himself, and the impossibility of your going far wrong if you humbly but heartily respect it.

Remember! It is Christianity TO DO GOOD always—even to those who do evil to us. It is Christianity to love our neighbour as ourself, and to do to all men as we would have them DO to us. It is Christianity to be gentle, merciful and forgiving, and to keep those qualities quiet in our own hearts, and never make a boast of them, or of our prayers or our love of God, but always to show that we love Him by humbly trying to do right in everything. If we do this, and remember the life and lessons of our Lord Jesus Christ, and try to act up to them, we may confidently hope that God will forgive us our sins and mistakes, and enable us to live and die in peace.

The Divine teacher was as gentle and considerate as He was powerful and wise. You all know He could still the raging of the sea, and could hush a little child. As the utmost results of the wisdom of men can only be at last to raise this earth to that condition to which His doctrine, untainted by the blindnesses and passions of men, would have exalted it long ago; so let us always remember that He has set us the example of blending the understanding and the imagination, and that, following it ourselves, we tread on His steps, and help our race onto its better and best days.

I have always striven in my writings to express veneration for the life and lessons of Our Saviour; because I feel it… But I have never made proclamation of this from the house tops.

NOTHING IS DISCOVERED WITHOUT GOD'S INTENTION AND ASSISTANCE, AND I SUPPOSE EVERY NEW KNOWLEDGE OF HIS WORKS THAT IS CONCEDED TO MAN TO BE DISTINCTLY A REVELATION BY WHICH MEN ARE TO GUIDE THEMSELVES.

DONNE, *John*

HOLY SONNETS

I

Thou has made me, and shall Thy works decay?
Repair me now, for now my hand doth haste,
I runne to death, and death meets me as fast,
And all my pleasures are like yesterday;

II

As due by many titles I resigne
My selfe to Thee, O God, first I was made
By Thee, and for Thee, and when I was decay'd
Thy blood bought that, the which was Thine;
I am Thy sonne, made with Thy selfe to shine.

IX

But who am I, that dare dispute with Thee
Oh God? Oh! Of thine onely worthy blood,
And drowne in it my sinnes black memorie;
That Thou remember them, some claime as debt,
I thinke it mercy if Thou wilt forget.

SERMON 3

For, if we consider God in the present, to day, now, God hath had as long a forenoone, as he shall have an afternoone; God has beene God, as many millions of millions of generations, already, as hee shall be hereafter; but if we consider man in the present, today, now, how short a forenoone hath any man had; if 60; if 80. Yeeres, yet few and evill have his daies beene. Nay if we take man collectively, entirely, altogether, all mankind, how short a forenoone hath man had? It is not yet 6000 yeeres, since man had his first being. But if we consider him in his Afternoone, in his future state, in his life after death, if every miniute of his 6000 yeeres, were multipli'd by so many millions of ages, all would amount to nothing, meerely nothing, in respect to that Eternity, which he is to dwell in. We can express man's Afternoone, his future Perpetuity, his everlastingnesse, but one way; But it is a faire way, a noble way; This; That how late a beginning soever God gave man, man shell no more see an end, no more die, than God Himselfe, that gave him life.

DOSTOEVSKY, *Fyodor Mikhailovich*

I have often and repeatedly prayed on my knees for a pure heart, and for a pure, sinless, calm, dispassionate style.

I PLACE MY TRUST IN GOD.

"My hour has come. I must die." To his little daughter and son he said: "Even if you should be so unhappy as to commit a crime in the course of your life, never despair of God. You are His children; humble yourselves before Him as before your father; implore His pardon, and He will rejoice over your repentance, as the father rejoiced over that of the prodigal son."

PEOPLE HERE ARE TRYING WITH ALL THEIR MIGHT TO WIPE ME OFF THE FACE OF THE EARTH FOR THE FACT THAT I PREACH GOD AND NATIONAL ROOTS.

DRYDEN, *John*

What weight of ancient witness can prevail
If private reason hold the public scale?
But, gracious God, how well dost Thou provide
For erring judgements an unerring guide!
Thy throne is darkness in th'abyss of light,
A blaze of glory that forbids the sight.
O teach me to believe Thee thus conceal'd,
And search no further than Thyself reveal'd.

ELIOT, *T. S.*

*We build in
vain unless the
Lord build
with us.*

Lord, shall we not bring these gifts to Your service?
Shall we not bring to Your service all our powers
For life, for dignity, grace and order,
And intellectual pleasures of the senses?
The Lord who created must wish us to create
And employ our creation again in His service
Which is already His service in creating.

O WEARINESS OF MEN WHO TURN FROM GOD

TO THE GRANDEUR OF YOUR MIND AND THE GLORY OF YOUR ACTION,

TO ARTS AND INVENTIONS AND DARING ENTERPRISES,

TO THE SCHEMES OF HUMAN GREATNESS THOROUGHLY DISCREDITED,

BINDING THE EARTH AND THE WATER TO YOUR SERVICE,

EXPLOITING THE SEAS AND DEVELOPING THE MOUNTAINS,

DIVIDING THE STARS INTO COMMON AND PREFERRED,

ENGAGED IN DEVISING THE PERFECT REFRIGERATOR,

ENGAGED IN WORKING OUT A RATIONAL MORALITY,

ENGAGED IN PRINTING AS MANY BOOKS AS POSSIBLE,

PLOTTING OF HAPPINESS AND FLINGING EMPTY BOTTLES,

TURNING FROM YOUR VACANCY TO FEVERED ENTHUSIASM

FOR NATION OR RACE OR WHAT YOU CALL HUMANITY;

THOUGH YOU FORGET THE WAY TO THE TEMPLE,

THERE IS ONE WHO REMEMBERS THE WAY TO YOUR DOOR:

LIFE YOU MAY EVADE, BUT DEATH YOU SHALL NOT.

YOU SHALL NOT DENY THE STRANGER.

EMERSON, *Ralph Waldo*

It now shows itself ethical and practical. We learn that God IS; that He is in me; and that all things are shadows of Him.

How dear, how soothing to man, arises the idea of God, peopling the lonely place, effacing the scars of our mistakes and disappointments! When we have broken our god of tradition, and ceased from our god of rhetoric, then may God fire the heart with His presence.

IF HE [MAN] WOULD KNOW WHAT THE GREAT GOD SPEAKETH, HE MUST "GO INTO HIS CLOSET AND SHUT THE DOOR," AS JESUS SAID.

In God every end is converted into a new means.

The ardors of piety agree at last with the coldest skepticism,—that nothing is of us or of our works,— that all is of God. Nature will not spare us the smallest leaf of laurel. All writing comes from the grace of God, and all doing and having. I would gladly be moral and keep all due meets and bounds, which I dearly love, and allow the most to the will of man; but I have set my heart on honesty in this chapter, and I can see nothing at last, in success or failure, than more or less of vital force supplied from the Eternal.

Our globe seen by God is a transparent law, not a mass of facts.

AS A PLANT UPON THE EARTH, SO A MAN RESTS UPON THE BOSOM OF GOD; HE IS NOURISHED BY UNFAILING FOUNTAINS AND DRAWS, AT HIS NEED, INEXHAUSTIBLE POWER.

FRANKLIN, *Benjamin*

HERE IS MY CREED. I BELIEVE IN ONE GOD, CREATOR OF THE UNIVERSE. THAT HE GOVERNS IT BY HIS PROVIDENCE. THAT HE OUGHT TO BE WORSHIPPED. THAT THE MOST ACCEPTABLE SERVICE WE RENDER TO HIM IS DOING GOOD TO HIS CHILDREN.

And conceiving God to be the fountain of wisdom, I thought it right and necessary to solicit His acceptance for obtaining it; to this end I formed the following little prayer, which was prefixed to my tables of examination, for daily use. O powerful Goodness! Bountiful Father! Merciful Guide! Increase in me that wisdom which discovers my truest interest. Strengthen my resolutions to perform that which wisdom dictates. Accept my kind offices to Thy other children as the only return in my power for Thy continual favours to me.

GOETHE, *Johann Wolfgang von*

General, natural religion, properly speaking, requires no faith, for the persuasion that a great producing, regulating and conducting Being conceals himself, as it were, behind nature, to make himself comprehensible to us. Such a conviction forces itself upon every one. Nay, if we for a moment let drop this thread, which conducts us through life, it may be immediately and everywhere resumed.

English, French, and Germans had attacked the Bible with more or less violence, acuteness, audacity, and wantonness, and just as often had it been taken under the protection of earnest, sound-thinking men of each nation. As for myself, I loved and valued it; for almost to it alone did I owe my moral culture: and the events, the doctrines, the symbols, the similes, had all impressed themselves deeply upon me and had influenced me in one way or another. These unjust, scoffing, and perverting attacks, therefore, disgusted me.

GOGOL, *Nikolai Vasilievich*

The Christian will show his humility before everyone, it is the first sign by which he may be recognized as a Christian.

LEAF THROUGH THE OLD TESTAMENT: THERE YOU WILL FIND EACH OF OUR PRESENT EVENTS, YOU WILL SEE MORE CLEARLY THAN DAY HOW THE PRESENT HAS SINNED BEFORE GOD, AND THE TERRIBLE JUDGMENT OF GOD UPON IT SO MANIFESTLY PRESENTED THAT THE PRESENT WILL SHAKE WITH TREMBLING.

The higher truths are, the more cautious one must be with them; otherwise they are converted into common things, and common things are not believed… The word must be treated honestly. It is the highest gift of God to man.

Great is the God who makes us wise. And how does He make us wise? By that very grief which we flee and from which we seek to hide ourselves.

Go on your knees before God and beg His wrath and His love! Wrath against what ruins man, love for the poor soul of the man who has been ruined and who ruins himself.

All the gifts of God are given to us so that we may serve our fellows.

HEINE, *Heinrich*

Faulting the Creator's not a
Thing befitting, as if clay
Would be wiser than the potter!

GOD HAS MADE OUR EYES A PAIR,

SO WE'D SEE CLEAR EVERYWHERE...

TWO EYES DID GOD GIVE LIKEWISE

SO WE'D LOOK AND GAPE AND STARE

AT THE WORLD HE MADE SO FAIR.

God's satire weighs on me. The great author of the universe, the Aristophanes of Heaven, was bent on demonstrating, with crushing force, to me, the little, earthly, German Aristophanes, how my wittiest sarcasms are only pitiful attempts at jesting in comparison with His, and how miserably I am beneath Him in humour, in colossal mockery.

HUGO, *Victor*

Cathedrals are beautiful

And rise high into the blue sky

But the nests of the swallows

Are the building of God.

Lord, I suffer much.
I cannot tell You
What goes on inside of me,
I cannot hide from You these dark battles,
The deep despair.
When God breathes on man, He opens his inner being
And sees deeply within it.

My Lord, my whole being is, since my childhood,
A hymn to the beauty of creation.

Let us rely on Him. Let us think and live on our knees;
Let us stop believing that we are wisdom, humility, light;
Let us not take one step without prayer,
Because our perfections will shine very little
After our death, before the star and the blue sky.
Only God can save us.

Let us love! That's all. This is God's will.

WE ARE DARKNESS

GOD ONLY IS THE ONLY BLUE NEEDED BY THE WORLD.

THE ABYSS WHILE TALKING TAKES THE ATOM AS WITNESS.

GOD ONLY IS GREAT! THIS IS THE PSALM OF THE BLADE OF GRASS;

GOD ONLY IS TRUE! IS THE HYMN OF THE PROUD WAVE;

GOD ONLY IS GOOD! IS THE SOUND OF THE WIND;

AH! DO NOT DELUDE YOURSELVES YOU LIVING.

KAFKA, *Franz*

Today the longing for God and the fear of sin are gravely enfeebled. We have sunk into a morass of presumption… Today there is no sin and no longing for God. Everything is completely mundane and utilitarian. God lies outside our existence. And therefore all of us suffer a universal paralysis of conscience. All transcendental conflicts seem to have vanished, and yet all of them defend themselves like the wooden figures of the Jacobskirche. We are immobilized. We are completely transfixed. More than that! Most of us are simply glued to the shaky stool of vulgar common sense by the filth of fear. That is our entire way of life.

LAMARTINE, *Alphonse*

I thought I understood everything; but then I realized that it is God who allows me, one of the most worthless intelligences, to understand.

Man should serve, love and fear God and he should put in him all of his thoughts and his hopes.

PROVIDENCE BRINGS TO THE SURFACE NEAR OUR REACH A WORLD OF TRUTHS JUST LIKE A FATHER LOWERS THE BRANCH TO BRING THE FRUIT NEAR TO THE SMALL HANDS OF HIS CHILD.

All true Christians, of all ranks and all places, and at all times pray to God. And the spirit prays and intercedes for them, and God accepts them.

God is, the ultimate good, ultimate beauty, Perfect Being, the Being over all beings.

LEOPARDI, *Giacomo*

If God is above morality, if good and

evil do not exist absolutely, etc., may

not God deceive us in what He has

revealed, promised, threatened, etc.

No, because He forbids deception.

THE TEN COMMANDMENTS CONTAIN GENERAL PRINCIPLES...CONCEIVED
FOR THE GOOD OF HUMANITY... THEY ARE INFINITE AND DIVERSE.

I consider God, not as superior to all the possible beings...but as having within
Himself all the possibilities, and existing in all the possible modes... His relation-
ships toward men and toward His creatures are perfectly convenient toward them;
they are therefore perfectly good, and better than those that other creatures have...
Thus, all religion remains standing, and the infinite perfection of God, that is
negated as being absolute, affirms itself as being relative, and as being perfect in the
order of things that we know, where the qualities that God has toward the world,
are relative to it, good and perfect.

LONGFELLOW, *Henry Wadsworth*

Wondrous truths, and manifold as
Wondrous,
God has written in those stars above;
But not less in the bright flowerets
Under us
Stands the revelation of His love.
Bright and glorious is that revelation,
Written all over this great world of
Ours....

LOWELL, *James Russell*

A PRAYER

God! do not let my loved one die,

But rather wait until the time

That I am grown in purity

Enough to enter Thy pure clime,

Then take me, I will gladly go,

So that my love remain below!

Oh let her stay! She is my birth

What I thought death must learn to be;

We need her more on our poor earth than

Thou canst need in Heaven with Thee;

She has her wings already, I

Must burst this earth—she'll ere I fly.

Then, God, take me! We shall be near,

More near than ever, each to each.

Her angel ears will find more clear

My heavenly than my earthly speech;

And still, as I draw nigh to Thee,

Her soul and mine shall closer be.

MANZONI, *Alessandro*

With faithful love

I come to Your holy throne,

I fall before Your presence,

My Judge, my King!

With what incomprehensible joy

I tremble before You!

I am dust and sin:

But look at him who implores You

Who wants Your forgiveness,

Who deserves, who worships,

Who gives thanks in me.

Look down merciful God,

You are mine; with You I breathe:
I live by You, Great God!
Mixed with Yours
I offer the love that's Yours.
Fulfill all my wishes;
To dust which will hear You,

Speak, and all will hear;
Give that all receives,

That will disappear before Your presence.

The heart wherein You dwell.

WHO SHAPED PLANTS' STEMS?
WHO CREATED THE BLOOMING WHEAT?
WHO MAKES LIFE FLOW IN THE VINE-SHOOT?
WHO PLACED IN GRAPES ITS TREASURE?
YOU, THE GREAT ONE, THE HOLY ONE, THE GOOD ONE,
THAT NOW BEING A GIFT—YOUR GIFT YOU RETAKE;
YOU, THAT IN EXCHANGE, WHAT AN EXCHANGE! YOU GIVE US
YOUR BODY, YOUR BLOOD, OH LORD,

EVEN THE HEARTS THAT WE OFFER YOU ARE YOURS:
AH! YOUR GIFT WAS BROKEN BY US;
BUT THE OTHER GOODNESS WHICH MADE THEM,
WILL RECEIVE THEM AS THEY ARE, TO MERCY;
AND WILL BREATHE ON THEM THE BREATH THAT CREATES
THAT FAITH THAT PASSES BEYOND ANY CURTAIN,
THAT HOPE WHICH DIES IN THE HEAVENS,
THAT LOVE WHICH WILL LIVE ETERNALLY WITH YOU.

MAZZINI, *Giuseppe*

Christianity is a (fixed) eternal religion, a unique religious synthesis.

Christianity is the formula of the individual, and as such is eternal and perfect to my thinking—for that formula no one can nullify.

GOD IS OUR DEFENCE, HE INCREASES OUR COURAGE AND RESOLUTION IN DIRECT PROPORTION TO THE MALEVOLENCE OF OUR ENEMIES…WE SAY WITH LUTHER.

I believe in God, in a Causative Intelligence superior to the created world.

(Letter to a friend)

I FEAR, DEAR FRIEND, THAT YOU ARE BENT TOO MUCH ON SELF-ANALYSIS, ON THINKING TOO MUCH OF YOUR SALVATION. LET GOD THINK OF IT; YOUR TASK IS TO ACT FOR THE FULFILMENT OF HIS LAW WHENEVER AND AS MUCH AS YOU CAN; TO PRAY AND WISH FERVENTLY FOR IT WHENEVER ACTION IS FORBIDDEN, AND TO TRUST HIM WITHOUT ANY TERMS... LOVE HIM IN A SIMPLE, UNEXACTING, UNSCRUTINIZING WAY AS A CHILD HIS MOTHER.

(Last words before his death)

Yes! Yes! I believe in God!

Above all beliefs, is God, the consciousness of an immortal soul, and the faith in other worlds nearer Him, in a necessary progress of ours towards God, in a virtue which must resist all temptations, in a constant sacrifice, in a love of the humanity in which He has placed us, in a worship of prayer, of affection, of sacred poetry.

MELVILLE, *German*

To Nathaniel Hawthorne (June 1851)

The reason the mass of men fear
God, and at the bottom dislike
Him, is because they rather
distrust His heart, and fancy Him
all brain like a watch.

Letter to Nathaniel Hawthorne (April 16, 1851)

We incline to think that God cannot explain His own
secrets, and that He would like a little information upon
certain points Himself. We mortals astonish Him as much as
He us. But it is this *Being* of the matter; there lies the knot
with which we choke ourselves. As soon as you say *Me*, a
God, a *nature*, so soon you jump off from your stool and
hang from a beam. Yes, that word is the hangman. Take God
out of the dictionary, and you would have Him in the street.

MILTON, *John*

We may be sure that
sufficient care has been
taken that the Holy Scriptures
should contain nothing unsuitable to the character or dignity of
God, and that God should say nothing of Himself which could
derogate from His own majesty.

LET US REQUIRE NO BETTER AUTHORITY THAN GOD HIMSELF FOR DETERMINING WHAT IS WORTHY OR UNWORTHY OF HIM.

Thee Father first they sung Omnipotent,
Immutable, Immortal, Infinite,
Eternal King; thee author of all being,
Fountain of light, thy self invisible
Amidst the glorious brightness where thou sit'st
Thron'd inaccessible, but when thou shad'st
The full blaze of thy beams, and through a cloud
Drawn round about thee like a radiant shrine,
Dark with excessive bright thy skirts appeer,
Yet dazle Heav'n, that brightest Seraphim
Approach not, but with both wings veil thir eyes.

If after the work of six days it be said of God that "he rested and was refreshed"... let us believe that it is not beneath the dignity of God...to be refreshed in that which refreshed Him... For however we may attempt to soften down such expressions by a latitude of interpretation, when applied to the Deity, it comes in the end to precisely the same.

PENN, *William*

Country life is to be preferred, for there we see the works of God; but in cities little else than the works of men.

Love is above all, and when it prevails in us all, we shall be lovely, and in love with God and one another.

AS PUPPETS ARE TO BABIES, AND BABIES TO CHILDREN, SO IS MAN'S WORKMANSHIP TO GOD'S; WE ARE THE PICTURE, HE'S THE REALITY.

God's works declare His power, wisdom, goodness; but man's works, for the most part, his pride, folly, and excess. The one is for the use, the other chiefly, for ostentation and lust.

Whatever else is done or omitted, be sure to begin and end with God.

Religion itself is nothing else but to love God and man.

PETRARCH, *Francesco*

Bowing one's knees to God, brings much benefit,

The knees and the mind

That your years preserves for much good.

HEAVENLY FATHER, AFTER LOST DAYS,
AFTER MANY WASTED NIGHTS
WITH THAT INTENSE DESIRE THAT BURNED INSIDE MY HEART,
LOOKING AT THE ACTIONS THAT FOR MY HARM ADORN IT,

MAY IT PLEASE YOU, WITH YOUR LIGHT, THAT I MAY RETURN
TO ANOTHER LIGHT AND TO MUCH BETTER ACCOMPLISHMENTS,
SO THAT IN SPITE OF TRAPS PREPARED BY HIM,
MY HARSH ADVERSARY MAY BE ASHAMED.
NOW ENDS, MY LORD THE ELEVENTH YEAR
THAT I WAS SUBJECTED TO MY CRUEL PUNISHMENT
THAT IS MOST BURDENSOME UPON THE MOST HUMBLE;

HAVE MERCY OF MY UNWORTHY SUFFERING
REMIND THEM HOW TODAY YOU WERE ON THE CROSS.

POPE, *Alexander*

Is the great chain,

that draws all to agree,

And drawn supports,

upheld by God, or Thee?

God, in the nature of each being, founds

Its proper bliss, and sets its proper bounds;

But as he framed the whole, the whole to bless,

On mutual wants built mutual happiness.

THAT CHAIN THAT LINKS TH'IMMENSE DESIGN,

JOINS HEAVEN AND EARTH, AND MORTAL AND DIVINE;

SEES THAT NO BEING ANY BLISS CAN KNOW,

BUT TOUCHES SOME ABOVE AND SOME BELOW.

Say first, of world above, or man below,
What can we reason, but from what we know?
Of man, what see we but his station here,
From which to reason, or to which refer?
Through worlds unnumber'd, tho' the God be known,
'Tis ours to trace Him only in our own.
He, who through vast immensity can pierce,
See worlds on worlds compose one universe,
Observe how system into system runs,
What other planets circle other suns...

PUSHKIN, *Alexander Sergeevich*

PURE MEN AND WOMEN TOO

Pure men and women too, all the world unspotted,
That they might fortify the heart against life's stress,
Composed such prayers as still comfort us and bless.
But none has stirred in me such deep emotions
As that the priest recites at Lententide devotions,
The words which mark for us that saddest season rise
Most often to my lips, and in that prayer lies
Support ineffable when I, a sinner, hear it:
Thou Lord my life, avert Thou from my spirit
Both idle melancholy and ambitious sting,
That hidden snake, and joy in foolish gossiping.
But let me see, O God, my sins, and make confession,
So that my brother be not damned by my transgression,
And quicken Thou in me the breath and being of
Both fortitude and meekness, chastity and love.

RABELAIS, *François*

When you say the word God, what does it mean to you? To me it means an Eternal Spirit who has no beginning, who has no end, such as no greater, no wiser or better can be conceived; By one act of His omnipotence He created all things, visible and invisible. His admirable wisdom regulates and governs the whole universe; His goodness nourishes and preserves all of His creation.

MAN MUST SERVE, LOVE AND FEAR GOD AND IN HIM HE MUST PUT ALL HIS THOUGHTS AND ALL HIS HOPES, AND BY HOPE SHAPED BY CHARITY HE MUST BOND WITH HIM SO THAT HE WILL NEVER BE DEFEATED BY SIN.

Let us pray to God the Creator, let us worship Him, let us rectify our faith in Him, let us glorify Him for His endless goodness.

What takes place is not what we wish or ask for, but what pleases Jesus Christ, our Lord whom God had established before the heavens were made...

We are all sinners and continually ask God to cleanse us of our sins.

RILKE, *Rainer Maria*

All love is an effort
for me, an outlay,
surmenage, only for
God have I any facility, for to
love God means to enter, to walk, to stand,
to rest and everywhere be in the love of God.

I know God has not placed us among the things to *choose*, but to employ our acceptance so fundamentally and so mightily that we can, in the end, receive nothing *but* the beautiful into our love, into our watchful attention, into our inextinguishable wonder.

FIRST YOU MUST FIND GOD SOMEWHERE, EXPERIENCE HIM AS INFINITELY, PRODIGIOUSLY, STUPENDOUSLY PRESENT, THEN WHETHER IT BE FEAR, OR ASTONISHMENT, OR BREATHLESSNESS, WHETHER IT BE, IN THE END, LOVE WITH WHICH YOU COMPREHEND HIM, IT HARDLY MATTERS AT ALL.

ROSSETTI, *Christina Georgina*

FROM "THE THREE ENEMIES"

THE FLESH

Sweet thou art pale.

More pale to see,

Christ hang upon a cruel tree

And bore His Father's wrath for me.

Sweet, thou art weary.

Not so Christ:

Whose mighty love of me suffic'd

For strength, Salvation, Eucharist.

THE WORLD

Sweet, thou art young.

So he was young

Who for my sake in silence hung

Upon the Cross with passion wrung.

Look thou art fair.

He was more fair

Than men, Who deign'd for me to wear

A visage marr'd beyond compare.

THE DEVIL

Thou drinkest deep.

When Christ would sup

He drain'd the dregs from out of my cup:

So how should I be lifted up?

Thou shalt have knowledge.

Helpless dust!

In Thee, O Lord, I put my trust:

Answer Thou for me, Wise and Just.

SHAKESPEARE, *William*

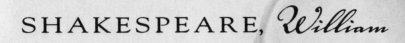

Now, God be praised,
that to believing souls,
Gives light in darkness,
comfort in despair!

GOD'S GREATNESS HATH BEEN GREAT TO THEE;

LET NEVER DAY NOR NIGHT UNHALLOW'D PASS,

BUT STILL REMEMBER WHAT THE LORD HATH DONE.

GOD SHALL BE MY HOPE,
MY STAY,
MY GUIDE, AND
LANTERN TO MY FEET.

God, *the best maker of all marriages,*
Combine your hearts in one.

We are in God's hand, brother.

In the name of God, I William Shakespeare…God be praised, do make and ordain this, my last will and testament in manner and form following. That is to say, first I commend my soul into the hands of God my Creator, hoping and assuredly believing, through the only merits of Jesus Christ, my saviour, to be made partaker of eternal life, and my body to the earth whereof it is made.

SHAW, *George Bernard*

O Lord our God arise!
All our salvation lies
In thy great hands.
Centre his thoughts on Thee,
Let him God's captain be,
Thine to eternity,
God save the King.

ALL LIFE IS A SERIES OF ACCIDENTS; BUT WHEN YOU FIND MOST OF THEM POINTING ALL ONE WAY, YOU MAY GUESS THAT THERE IS SOMETHING BEHIND THEM THAT IS NOT AN ACCIDENT.

I am ready to admit after contemplating the world and human nature for nearly sixty years, I see no other way out of the world's misery but the way which would have been found by Christ's will if he had undertaken the work of a modern practical statesman.

I believe that there is somebody behind the somebody. All bodies are products of the life force.

SOLZHENITSYN, *Alexander*

A PRAYER

How easy it is for me to live with Thee Lord! How easy to believe in Thee! When my thoughts pull back in puzzlement or go soft, when the brightest people see no further than this evening and know not what to do tomorrow, Thou sendest down to me clear confidence that Thou art, and will make sure that not all the ways of the good are closed. On this ridge of earthly fame, I look back in wonder at the road which I would never have been able to divine alone—that wonderous path through hopelessness to this ridge from which I too have been able to radiate among men a reflection of Thy rays. And Thou will grant me to continue reflecting them as long as need be. And that which I cannot complete will mean that Thou hast allotted it to others.

STOWE, *Harriet Beecher*

GOD ALWAYS
MAKES MOST
PROSPEROUS
THOSE WHO ARE
MOST OBEDIENT
TO HIS LAWS IN
THE BIBLE.

I think the All Wise often thinks beyond the words of our prayers and gives us the real thing.

Still, still with Thee, when the purple morning breaketh,
When the bird waketh and the shadows flee;
Fairer than morning, lovelier than the daylight,
Dawns the sweet consciousness, I am with Thee!

He [Harriet's brother] and I are Christ worshippers, adoring Him as the Image of the invisible God.

MY GOD IS MY EVER PRESENT MEDIUM OF COMMUNICATION WITH THE UNSEEN, AND COMMUNION WITH HIM IS THE FIRMEST OF REALITIES TO ME.

For who is this Jesus? Not a man who died eighteen hundred years ago; but a living God, who claims at this moment to be the Prince of the kings of the earth—to be the great reigning and working Force, who must reign till He has put all things under His feet.

SWIFT, *Jonathan*

God's mercy is over all his works.

MISERABLE MORTALS! HOW CAN WE CONTRIBUTE TO THE HONOUR AND GLORY OF GOD? I WISH THAT EXPRESSION WERE STRUCK OUT OF OUR PRAYER-BOOKS.

TASSO, *Torquato*

TO OUR LORD

Father in heaven, now that another cloud the road
Effectively hides, and wrong ways I take
With uncertain walk among this unstable field
Of the worldly and marshy valley,

Sustain with Your holy hand, keep from failing
My erring way, and by Your mercy the light
Sweet over me shine, and for an escape
Show me the path that I had left behind.

I pray You, allow my hair to be covered
With white snow, and that my day of birth
Close in eternal gloominess the waning light,

Give me that I may return to your house,
As angel sublime that rises and flies
From base marshy clay with wings to heaven.

TENNYSON, *Alfred*

Hallowed be Thy name—Hallelujah!

Infinite Ideality!

Immeasurable Reality!

Infinite Personality!

Hallowed be Thy name—Hallelujah!

We feel we are nothing—for all is Thou and Thee;
We feel we are something—that also has come from Thee;
We know we are nothing—but Thou will help us be.
Hallowed be Thy name.—Hallelujah!

WHEN MOSES ON THE MOUNTAIN'S BROW
HAD MET THE ETERNAL FACE TO FACE,
WHILE ANXIOUS ISRAEL STOOD BELOW,
WONDERING AND TREMBLING AT ITS BASE;
HIS VISAGE AS HE DOWNWARD TROD,
SHONE STARLIKE ON THE SHRINKING CROWD,
WITH LUSTRE BORROWED FROM HIS GOD:
THEY COULD NOT BROOK IT AND THEY BOWED.
THE MERE REFLECTION OF THE BLAZE
THAT LIGHTENED ROUND CREATION'S LORD,
WAS SO PUISSANT FOR THEIR GAZE;
AND HE THAT CAUGHT IT WAS ADORED.

THEN HOW INEFFABLY AUGUST,
HOW PASSING WONDROUS MUST HE BE,
WHOSE PRESENCE LENT TO EARTHLY DUST
SUCH PERMANENCE OF BRILLIANCY!

Fear not the hidden purpose
of that Power which alone is great.
Nor the Myriad world, His shadow,
nor the silent Opener of the Gate.

TENNYSON *(cont.)*

Where is the wonderful abode,
The holy, secret, searchless shrine,
Where dwells the immaterial God,
The all-pervading and benign.
O! that He were revealed to me,
Fully and palpably displayed
In all the awful majesty
Of heaven's consummate pomp arrayed.

My Father and my Brother and my God!
Touch me with sorrow! Soften me with grief!
Until this battled wall of unbelief
Built around my warring spirit fall away!
Then take me to thyself—a full-eared-sheaf
Ripe for the harvest on an autumn day.

IF GOD WERE

TO WITHDRAW

HIMSELF FOR A

MOMENT FROM

THE UNIVERSE

EVERYTHING

WOULD

VANISH INTO

NOTHINGNESS.

Take away belief in the self-conscious personality of God and you will take away the backbone of the world.

THOREAU, *Henry David*

When God made man, he reserved some parts and some rights to himself—the eye has many qualities which belong to God more than man—It is lightening which flashes in them—When I look into my companion's eye, I think it is God's mine. It is a noble feature—it cannot be degraded. For God can look on all things undefiled.

WHY, GOD, DID YOU INCLUDE ME IN YOUR GREAT SCHEME? WILL YOU NOT MAKE ME A PARTNER AT LAST?

I thank God for sorrow—It is hard to be abused—Is not he kind still—who lets the south wind blow—this warm sun shine on me?

What if you or I be dead—God is alive still.

TOLSTOY, *Leo*

PRAYER
Oh God, God inconceivable…
I have erred… I knew that I was
going astray…but I never forgot
Thee. I always felt Thy presence
even in the very moment of my
sins. I all but lost Thee, but Thou
hast…saved me!

THE LONGER WE LIVE THE MORE CLEARLY AND FULLY DO WE LEARN THE
WILL OF GOD, AND IN CONSEQUENCE WHAT WE MUST DO TO FULFILL IT.

God and the soul are known by me in the
same way I know infinity: not by means of
definitions but in quite another way… Just as
I know assuredly that there is an infinity of
numbers so do I know that there is a God.

Does truth cease to be truth because
the men who professed it become
weak under the pressure of torture?
That which is of God must conquer
that which is of man.

Traditions may proceed from men and be false; but
reason indubitably comes from God.

THERE WILL BE THE THING WHICH OUGHT TO BE, THAT WHICH IS WELL-PLEASING TO GOD, WHICH IS ACCORDING TO THE LAW HE HAS PUT IN OUR HEART AND REVEALED TO OUR MINDS.

Yet another effort, and the Galilean will conquer. Not in that ruthless sense understood by the pagan emperor, but in that true sense in which He Himself spoke of His conquest of the world.

He has actually overcome the world.

Each will have to make his own choice: to oppose the will of God, building upon the sands the unstable house of his brief illusive life, or to join in the eternal, deathless movement of true life in accordance with God's will.

THE SOLUTION BEFORE US IS…BY NOTHING ELSE THAN A FORWARD MOVEMENT ALONG THAT ROAD WHICH THE LAW OF CHRIST POINTS OUT TO THE HEARTS OF MEN.

For life is life only when it is the carrying out of God's purpose. But by opposing Him, people deprive themselves of life, and at the same time, neither for one year, nor for one hour, can they delay the accomplishment of God's purpose.

WORDSWORTH, *William*

Glory to God...

All things counter, original, spare, strange;

Whatever is fickle, freckled (who knows how?)

With swift, slow; sweet, sour; adazzle, dim;

He Fathers — forth whose beauty is past change;

Praise Him.

STERN LAWGIVER! YET THOU DOST WEAR

THE GODHEAD MOST BENIGNANT GRACE;

NOR KNOW WE ANYTHING SO FAIR

AS IS THE SMILE UPON THY FACE;

FLOWERS LAUGH BEFORE THEE ON THEIR BEDS;

AND FRAGRANCE IN THY FOOTING TREADS;

THOU DOST PRESERVE THE STARS FROM WRONG;

AND THE ANCIENT HEAVENS, THROUGH THEE, ARE

FRESH AND STRONG.

TO HUMBLER FUNCTIONS, AWFUL POWER!

I CALL THEE: I MYSELF COMMEND

UNTO THY GUIDANCE FROM THIS HOUR;

OH LET MY WEAKNESS HAVE AN END!

GIVE UNTO ME, MADE LOWLY WISE,

THY SPIRIT OF SELF SACRIFICE;

THE CONFIDENCE OF REASON GIVE;

AND IN THE LIGHT OF TRUTH THY BONDMAN LET ME LIVE!

BIOGRAPHIES

1265–1321

ALIGHIERI, DANTE

The greatest poet of the Renaissance. Also a prose writer, literary theorist, moral philosopher, and political thinker. Wrote many important works such as *The New Life*, *Il Convivio*, and *De Monarchia*. His greatest work, the Christian epic *The Divine Comedy*, is considered to be one of the landmarks in world literature.

1685–1750

BACH, JOHANN SEBASTIAN

German composer born to a family of renowned musicians. Composer of many famed orchestral works, chief of which are his *Brandenburg Concertos*. Bach specialized in church music and composed 265 cantatas. He also wrote extensively for the organ and harpsichord. Today he is considered to be one of history's greatest composers.

1561–1626

BACON, FRANCIS

Lord chancellor of England, philosopher, essayist, and statesman. Was a foremost representative of British empirical philosophy. He stressed the importance of observation in scientific enquiry. Wrote *The Advancement of Learning* and *Novum Organum*, which led to the development of modern science. A man of letters whose *Essays* and other writings mark him as a master of English prose.

BEETHOVEN, LUDWIG VAN

German musical composer and creator of unparalleled original music. Composed many great works, chief among which are nine magnificent symphonies, the *Moonlight* and *Appassionata* sonatas, the opera *Fidelio*, the *Rasoumoffsky Quartets*, and two superb masses. While totally deaf, he composed the magnificent *Ninth Symphony*. His music is considered to have reached heights never exceeded since.

1770—1827

BLAKE, WILLIAM

English painter, poet, engraver, and visionary mystic. Considered one of the earliest and most important figures of the Romantic Movement. Wrote and illustrated his own books. Blake's favorite subjects were scenes from the Bible and Dante's works. Some of his finest works are *The Marriage of Heaven and Hell*, *Visions of the Daughters of Albion*, and *Songs of Innocence and Experience*.

1757—1827

BRAHE, TYCHO

Danish astronomer. Made accurate astronomical measurements of more than seven hundred stars. His unprecedented accuracy in celestial observations, together with equipment given to him by royalty, led to compilation of data that helped his pupil Johann Kepler to formulate the laws of planetary motion. The data gathered by Brahe were the best available until the invention of the telescope in the seventeenth century.

1546—1601

1818—1848

BRONTË, EMILY

English novelist and poet. Considered by some to be the greatest of the Brontë sisters. Wrote the highly imaginative novel *Wuthering Heights*. Little is known about her because of her reserved life. Her contributions in the area of poetry indicate, according to some, true poetic genius.

1806—1861

BROWNING, ELIZABETH BARRETT

English poet and wife of famed English poet Robert Browning. Known predominantly for her love poems. Wrote *Sonnets from the Portuguese*, but her most ambitious work was *Aurora Leigh*, which became a huge popular success. Spent the last years of her life in Italy, where she died in her husband's arms.

1812—1889

BROWNING, ROBERT

Major English poet of the Victorian age. His greatest work was *The Ring and the Book*. Also wrote *Paracelsus*, *Sordello*, and a great number of poems. Married Elizabeth Barrett, with whom he had a very happy marriage. In his last years, wrote long narrative and dramatic poems often dealing with contemporary themes. Influenced many modern poets such as Robert Frost and Ezra Pound.

BRUNO, GIORDANO

Italian Renaissance philosopher, astronomer, and mathematician whose theories anticipated modern science. Burned at the stake after being declared a heretic. Saw God as the only reality. Wrote metaphysical works, dialogues, satire, and poetry. Stands as one of the most important figures in the history of Western thought.

1548?–1600

BUONARROTI, MICHELANGELO

Italian sculptor, painter, and architect who was one of the great titans of the Italian Renaissance. In sculpture, architecture, painting, and poetry, he had a great influence on his contemporaries and Western art in general. Created some of the world's greatest masterpieces. He painted the Sistine Chapel ceiling and *The Last Judgment*. He sculpted the great *David*, *Moses*, and *The Pieta*. He also composed many remarkable sonnets.

1475–1564

CAMPANELLA, TOMMASO

Platonic philosopher, poet, and writer. Sought to reconcile Renaissance humanism with Roman Catholic theology. Best remembered for his work *Città del Sole*, written while he was a prisoner of the Spanish Inquisition. While in prison, he wrote poetry that is considered to be the most original of the period. He also wrote a collection of thirty books titled *Theologia*.

1568–1639

CÉZANNE, PAUL

French painter and one of the greatest Post-Impressionists. Influenced many other artists and the cubism movement. Specialized mostly in landscapes and still lifes. Created many masterpieces such as *The Mills of Gardane*, *The Card Players*, and *The Boy in a Red Waist Coat*.

1839—1906

CHAUCER, GEOFFREY

English poet. Considered to be the greatest English poet preceding Shakespeare. Traveled across Europe as an English diplomat. Wrote *Book of the Duchesse*, an elegy for the Duchess of Lancaster; *Hours of Fame*, a love vision narrative poem; and the romance *Troylus and Criseyde*. His greatest work is his unfinished masterpiece, *Canterbury Tales*, ranked as one of the greatest poetic works in English.

1340?—1400

CHEKHOV, ANTON PAVLOVICH

Major Russian playwright, foremost master of the modern short story, and a major representative of the Russian realist school of the late nineteenth century. Some of his greatest masterpieces are *The Seagull*, *Uncle Vanya*, *Three Sisters*, and *The Cherry Orchard*. Today he is chiefly known for his plays, but critical opinion increasingly views his stories as greater.

1860—1904

COPERNICUS, NICOLAUS

1473—1543

Polish astronomer. Famous for being the proponent of the idea that the earth rotates around its axis and around the sun. Wrote the *Commentariolus*, a manuscript summary of his theory, and later his complete work *De Revolutionibus Orbum Celestium*. His views had a profound impact on science and philosophy.

DA VINCI, LEONARDO

1452—1519

Italian painter, sculptor, architect, and engineer. Revolutionized Italian painting by emphasizing soft transitions in light. In science, he anticipated the invention of planes and submarines. Executed some of the finest anatomical drawings ever achieved. Painted the famed *Mona Lisa* and *The Last Supper*. He is considered to be one of the greatest geniuses of all time.

DEFOE, DANIEL

1659?—1731

English novelist and political writer. His publication of *The Review* was a landmark in English journalism. Wrote the world-famous *Robinson Crusoe*, *Moll Flanders*, *Roxana*, and *Journal of the Plague Years*. His style is said to have been influenced by the Bible, John Bunyan, and the pulpit oratory of the day.

DELACROIX, EUGÈNE

French painter. Major proponent of the French Romantic Movement. His use of colors influenced both Impressionism and Post-Impressionism. His inspiration came chiefly from historical and contemporary events. Some of his most famous masterpieces are *Dante and Virgil in Hell*, *Liberty Leading the People*, and *Death at Sardanapalus*.

1798—1863

DELEDDA, GRAZIA

Novelist and writer of the "Verismo" (Naturalistic) school of Italian literature. Was awarded the Nobel Prize for literature in 1926. One of her favorite themes was the effect of temptation and sin among primitive human beings. Her most important works are *Dopo il Divorzio* (After the Divorce), *Elias Portolu*, and *Cenere* (Ashes).

1875—1936

DESCARTES, RENÉ

French philosopher and mathematician. Also called Cartesius. Founded modern philosophy and was one of the world's most influential thinkers. His foundational principle is expressed in his statement "I think; therefore, I am." Believed God's existence to be a self-evident truth. Made significant contributions to physical sciences.

1596—1650

DICKENS, CHARLES

Considered to be the greatest English novelist of the Victorian era. Heavily interested in social injustices and dedicated to producing social reforms. Wrote world-famous works such as *Oliver Twist*, *A Christmas Carol*, *David Copperfield*, *Great Expectations*, and *A Tale of Two Cities*. Ranked by some as the greatest English novelist.

1812—1870

DONNE, JOHN

Leading poet of the metaphysical school and dean of Saint Paul Cathedral in London. Started with lyric poetry. Later he wrote intensely religious poetry and became known for his eloquent sermons. Had a powerful influence on the writers of the seventeenth and twentieth centuries. Wrote *Devotions upon Emergent Occasions*, *Biathanatos*, and *Essays on the Divinity*.

1573—1631

DOSTOEVSKY, FYODOR MIKHAILOVICH

Russian novelist, journalist, and short-story writer. His novels explore human freedom, the justification of religion, and psychological conflicts. Among his greatest works are *Crime and Punishment* and *The Brothers Karamazov*. His understanding of the dark side of the human mind and his profound insights greatly influenced the twentieth-century novel.

1821—1881

DRYDEN, JOHN

English poet, critic, and dramatist. Made poet laureate by Charles II. Wrote several plays such as *The Indian Princess*, *The Conquest of Granada*, and *Auren-Zebe*. Known primarily as a poet. Author of "Ode for St. Cecilia's Day," "Alexander's Feast," and "Ode to the Memory of Mrs. Anne Killigrew."

1631—1700

DÜRER, ALBRECHT

The most famous German artist of Renaissance Germany. Excelled in painting, drawing, and print-making. Wrote useful theoretical writings on art, all of which had a strong influence on sixteenth-century artists in Germany and the lowlands. Traveled to Italy and studied under the great Italian master Bellini. Some of his greatest works are *Madonna of the Rose Garlands*, *The Adoration of the Trinity*, *St. Jerome in His Study*, and *Melancolia*. He is widely recognized as one of the greatest artists of the Northern Renaissance.

1471—1528

EINSTEIN, ALBERT

German-American physicist. Most famous for conceiving the general theory of relativity. Also contributed a mathematical description of Brownian movement and the quantum theory. Was awarded the Nobel Prize in physics in 1921. His scientific contributions are recognized as the most important of the twentieth century.

1879—1955

ELIOT, T. S.

American-British poet. A leader of the Modernist movement in poetry. He was very influential over twentieth-century culture in the period between the two world wars. Received the Nobel Prize for literature in 1948. Some of his best poetic works are "Prufock and Other Observations," "Poems," and "The Waste Land." Among his best-known plays in verse are *Murder in the Cathedral*, *Family Reunion*, *The Cocktail Party*, and *The Elder Statesman*.

1888–1965

EMERSON, RALPH WALDO

American poet, essayist, lecturer, and the leading exponent of New England transcendentalists. Known for his inspirational writings such as *Nature* and *The American Scholar*. Some of his best-known poetic works are "Brahma," "The Rhodora," and "Condor Hymn." His works stressed, above all, the spiritual potential of man.

1803–1882

FARADAY, MICHAEL

English scientist. As a result of his experiments in the field of electrodynamics, he is considered to be the founder of that field. He discovered some of the basic laws of electrolysis and discovered benzene. Two electrical units, the farad and the faraday, were named after him.

1791–1867

FICHTE, JOHANN GOTTLIEB

German philosopher and disciple of Immanuel Kant. One of the greatest transcendental idealists. Believed that knowledge and love of God were the end of life and that the divine order of the universe was the highest aspect of the life of reason. Wrote *The Vocations of Man*, *The Characteristics of the Present Age*, and *The Way toward the Blessed Life*.

1762—1814

FRANKLIN, BENJAMIN

American statesman, scientist, philosopher, inventor, publisher, and scientist. Spent much time in scientific pursuits. Helped draft the Declaration of Independence, of which he was a signer, and helped draw up the U. S. Constitution. At the end of the Revolutionary War, he was one of the diplomats chosen to negotiate peace with Britain. He also contributed to science with his experiments in electricity.

1706—1790

GALILEI, GALILEO

Italian scientist, mathematician, astronomer, and physicist. Considered a founder of the experimental method. Supported the Copernican Theory and was declared a heretic as a result. His major works are *Dialogue Concerning Two Chief World Systems* and *Dialogue Concerning Two New Sciences*. Proposed the law of uniform acceleration for falling bodies, developed the astronomical telescope, discovered craters on the moon, and showed that the Milky Way is composed of stars.

1564—1642

GLUCK, CHRISTOPH WILLIBALD VON

German composer. After producing operas in current styles for twenty years, he produced the revolutionary *Orfeo* and *Euridice*, characterized by simplicity, naturalism, and an emphasis on drama rather than vocal virtuosity. Composed the operas *Alceste*, *Iphigenio*, and *Aulide*, which departed from tradition because French librettos were used. Influenced Mozart and Cherubini.

1714—1787

GOETHE, JOHANN WOLFGANG VON

German poet, novelist, playwright, and natural philosopher. The greatest figure of the German Romantic Movement. His greatest work, *Faust*, dramatizes the battle between good and evil and is considered to be the greatest masterpiece in German literature. His written works are contained in 133 volumes (Weimar edition).

1749—1832

GOGOL, NIKOLAI VASILIEVICH

Ukrainian-born Russian humorist, dramatist, and novelist. By writing *Dead Souls*, considered to be his masterpiece, and *The Overcoat*, he established the foundations of the great nineteenth-century tradition of Russian realism. Preaching and pleasing God were his first aims until the end of his life. Believed that God had endowed him with literary talent to teach the Russians the righteous way of living in an unrighteous world.

1809—1852

HANDEL, GEORGE FRIDERIC

German composer. Combined German and Italian styles, and later English and French. Composed successfully in Italy and England. Wrote forty-six operas and then moved to compose oratorios. Among his best are *Israel in Egypt* and *Samson and Jeptha*. His most-loved oratorio remains his *Messiah*. Was particularly appreciated by the British people for his sense of charity and concern for other people.

1685—1759

HARVEY, WILLIAM

English physician who discovered the true nature of the circulation of blood and of the heart as a pump. Was appointed physician extraordinary to the king. His major works are *On the Motion of the Heart* and *Blood of Animals*. Harvey's exacting scientific method of research influenced scientific research for generations.

1578—1657

HAYDN, FRANZ JOSEPH

Austrian composer. Wrote eighty-five string quartets and 104 symphonies. While visiting London, he composed the two greatest works of his old age: *The Creation* and *The Seasons*. In 1797, he wrote *The Emperor's Hymn*, which became Austria's national anthem. Has been called the father of symphony for his development of symphonic form and orchestration.

1732—1809

1770—1831

HEGEL, GEORG WILHELM FRIEDRICH

German idealist philosopher who created the dialectical scheme: that thesis and antithesis will lead to synthesis. He influenced the development of existentialism, positivism, and analytic philosophy. Some of his great works are *The Phenomenology of the Mind*, *The Science of Logic*, and *The Philosophy of Right*. Taught that matter was the counterpart of spirit. Was one of the foremost exponents of idealism.

1797—1856

HEINE, HEINRICH

German-Jewish poet. Wrote *Romanzero*, which contains some of his finest poems, and *Poems 1853–1854*, considered to be of the same caliber. Accepted the idea of a personal God after falling gravely ill. Wrote many satires in prose and poetry on German life and the unfairnesses of the social order. His works were banned during the Nazi regime.

1802—1885

HUGO, VICTOR

French poet, novelist, and playwright whose very large works contributed abundantly to the Romantic Movement. Wrote several well-appreciated volumes of lyric poetry and outstanding works such as *The Hunchback of Notre Dame*, *Le Roi S'amuse*, and *Le Feuilles D'automne*. Provided the subjects for Verdi's operas *Rigoletto* and *Ernani*. He is considered one of the finest French poets.

INGRES, JEAN AUGUSTE DOMINIQUE

Leader of the French tradition of neoclassical painting after Jacques Louis David. Heavily influenced by Raphael, he was the leading classicist of his period and an excellent draftsman. His works are today found in some of the world's greatest museums. Because of his fame, he was made a lifelong senator and received many honors. Some of his greatest works are *Turkish Women at the Bath* and great portraits such as *Mme. Poitessier* and *La Comtesse D'Haussonville*.

1842—1910

JAMES, WILLIAM

American philosopher and psychologist who developed the philosophy of pragmatism. His monumental *Principles of Psychology* established him as one of the greatest thinkers of his time. Other major works are *The Will to Believe*, *Essays in Popular Philosophy*, *Human Immortality*, and *The Varieties of Religious Experience*.

1883—1924

KAFKA, FRANZ

Czech-born German-Jewish writer of visionary fiction that expresses the anxieties of twentieth-century man. In philosophy, Kafka is akin to the Danish thinker Sören Kierkegaard and to twentieth-century existentialists. His work has the qualities both of expressionism and of surrealism. His best works are *The Judgment*, *The Castle*, and *The Metamorphoses*. His writings were rediscovered after World War II and had a strong influence on German literature and modern writers.

KANT, IMMANUEL

German metaphysician and philosopher whose work in the theory of knowledge, ethics, and aesthetics had a very strong influence on subsequent philosophy. His greatest works are *Critique of Pure Reason*, *Critique of Practical Reason*, *Critique of Judgment*, and *Religion within the Boundaries of Pure Reason*. In addition to these, he also wrote various scientific works. He is considered to be one of the greatest modern thinkers.

1724—1804

KEPLER, JOHANN

German astronomer and natural philosopher known for formulating and verifying the three laws of planetary motion. These laws are now known as Kepler's laws. He discovered that the earth and planets travel about the sun in elliptical orbits, thus transforming the old description of the heavens. He became imperial mathematician and court astronomer to Rudolf II, Holy Roman emperor. His greatest works are *Tabulae Rudolphinae* and *Admonitio and Astronomos*.

1571—1630

KIERKEGAARD, SÖREN

Danish religious philosopher and critic of rationalism. Regarded as the founder of existential philosophy. Kierkegaard's influence was at first confined to Scandinavia and to German-speaking Europe, where his work had a strong impact on Protestant theology and on Austrian novelist Franz Kafka. As existentialism developed into a European movement, Kierkegaard's work was widely translated, and he was recognized as one of the important figures of modern culture. Wrote *Either Or*, *Stages of Life's Way*, *Fear and Trembling*, *Works of Love*, and *Christian Discourses*.

1813—1855

LAMARTINE, ALPHONSE

French poet, man of letters, and statesman who was one of the leaders of the Romantic Movement. Known chiefly for his poetry. His most influential volume of poetry is *Mèditations Poètiques*. Was also a prolific writer. Wrote *Histoire de Girondins* and the autobiographical novels *Raphael* and *Graziella*.

1790—1869

LEIBNIZ, GOTTFRIED WILHELM VON

German philosopher and mathematician. Important as a metaphysician, a logician, and for inventing differential and integral calculus. In metaphysics he conceived a system in which substance consists of atoms that form a preestablished, perfect harmony with God as Creator. Among his works are his *New Essays, On Human Understanding, The Theodicee*, and *Monadologie*.

1646—1716

LEOPARDI, GIACOMO

Considered by some to be one of Italy's greatest poets. By age twenty, he had written several outstanding odes, including "On a Monument to Dante." Leopardi first attracted public notice with his patriotic ode "All'Italia" (To Italy). Today he is known as the greatest lyric poet of nineteenth-century Italy. *Operette Morali* is his outstanding prose work. He is best known for his lyrical odes.

1798—1837

LISZT, FRANZ

Hungarian virtuoso and composer. Aside from his achievements as pianist and conductor, Liszt taught more than four hundred pupils, turned out some 350 compositions, and wrote or collaborated on eight volumes of prose, not counting his correspondence. Among his best works are twelve symphonic poems, two piano concertos, and several sacred choral works. He influenced the music of his times and anticipated many developments.

1811—1886

LONGFELLOW, HENRY WADSWORTH

American nineteenth-century poet. During his lifetime, he was considered to be one of the most popular American poets. Longfellow's contemporaries praised his poetry for its clarity and simplicity. Recognition as a poet came with his *Voices in the Night*, followed by *Ballads and Other Poems*. He is one of the most loved American poets.

1807—1882

LOWELL, JAMES RUSSELL

American poet, essayist, editor, diplomat, and critic best known for his poetry. Opposed the Mexican War and slavery. His works include *A Fable for Critics*, *The Vision of Sir Launfal*, *Biglow Papers*, and *My Study Windows*. His volumes of verse include *Under the Willows*, *The Cathedral*, *Three Memorial Poems*, *Hearts Ease and Rue*, and *Political Essays*.

1819—1891

1785–1873

MANZONI, ALESSANDRO

Italian novelist. Wrote several tragedies and some poetry. His most famous work is the greatly loved *The Betrothed*, which made him the leading Italian romanticist and is ranked among the masterpieces of world literature. Also wrote *Sacred Hymns*, *Adelchi*, and *Il Conte di Carmagnola*. Was revered by men of his time and made senator in 1860.

1863–1945

MASCAGNI, PIETRO

Italian composer and representative of "verismo" in operatic music. Studied at the Milan Conservatory, conducted for a traveling opera company, and taught piano. His first opera, *Cavalleria Rusticana*, won a major musical competition and became world famous. His other successful operas are *L'Amico Fritz* and *Iris*. He often conducted his own works.

1805–1872

MAZZINI, GIUSEPPE

Italian writer, lawyer, and patriot. Considered to have played an indispensible part in the creation of the Italian nation. For years he struggled to find ways to fuse the Italian states into one and inspired many in the pursuit of unity and freedom. His love for the Bible and Christ played a fundamental role in his personal life and political philosophy.

1819—1891

MELVILLE, HERMAN

American novelist, short-story writer, and poet. Best known for his novels of the sea. Wrote the masterpiece *Moby Dick*. Also wrote *Typee: A Peep at Polynesian Life*, *Omoo: A Narrative of Adventures in the South Seas*, and *Mardi and a Voyage Thither*. These and other novels contributed to making him the most celebrated American writer.

1806—1873

MILL, JOHN STUART

English philosopher, economist, and political scientist. His major publications are *A System of Logic* and *Principles of Political Economy*. Also wrote *Three Essays on Religion* and *On Liberty*. Made important contributions to inductive logic. Did much reform work, helped the poor, and advocated universal suffrage and franchise.

1608—1674

MILTON, JOHN

English poet who had a powerful influence on succeeding poets. Dedicated to the defense of civil and religious liberty. Authored pastoral poems and political works. His greatest work is *Paradise Lost*, considered to be one of the world's greatest masterpieces. Twelve books long, it describes Satan's revolt against God and the fall of man. Also wrote the sequel, *Paradise Regained*, and high-caliber sonnets in Petrarchan form in both Italian and English.

MOZART, WOLFGANG AMADEUS

Austrian composer. Began playing the clavier by age three and composing by five. Toured Europe as a pianist at six. By age eight his first symphonies were published. Wrote musical masterpieces throughout his life. His most famous works are his operas *The Marriage of Figaro*, *Don Giovanni*, *Così Fan Tutte*, and *The Magic Flute*. Also wrote the *Jupiter* and *Coronation* symphonies. Was a master in every field of music.

1756—1791

NEWTON, SIR ISAAC

English mathematician, physicist, and philosopher. One of the leading pioneers of science. Had a revolutionary influence on man's view of the physical world. He enunciated his universal laws of gravitation and motion. Made important contributions to the corpuscular theory of light, the construction of the telescope, and other works in optics. Discovered calculus at the same time as Leibniz. His chief works are the *Principia* and *Optics*.

1642—1727

PASCAL, BLAISE

French mathematician, physicist, religious philosopher, and writer who was the founder of the modern theory of probabilities. Influenced other thinkers such as Rousseau, Bergson, and the existentialists. His major works are *Les Provinciales* and *Pensées*. Pascal is considered one of the great minds in Western intellectual history.

1623—1662

PASTEUR, LOUIS

World-renowned French chemist and biologist who founded the science of microbiology, proved the germ theory of disease, invented the process of pasteurization, and developed vaccines for several diseases, including rabies. His major works are *Oeuvres Completes* and *Correspondence*. By the time of his death, Pasteur had become a national hero.

1822—1895

PENN, WILLIAM

English Quaker leader and advocate of religious freedom who founded Pennsylvania. Was jailed in the Tower of London for having published the religious tract *The Sandy Foundation Shaken*. During his imprisonment, he wrote his most famous book, *No Cross, No Crown*. Later, in Newgate Prison, he wrote *The Great Case of the Liberty of Conscience* in defense of religious tolerance.

1644—1718

PETRARCH, FRANCESCO

Italian scholar, poet, and humanist whose poems addressed to Laura, an idealized beloved, contributed to lyric poetry in the Renaissance. Regarded as the greatest scholar of his age. His humanist ideas were a major contributor to the development of the Renaissance. His major works are *De Vita Solitaria*, *De Otio Religioso*, *Rime*, and *Metricae*.

1304—1374

1463–1494

PICO DELLA MIRANDOLA, GIOVANNI

Italian Renaissance scholar and humanist philosopher. Belonged to the group of Florentine humanists and was noted for great learning. Wrote an eloquent essay on human dignity. He also wrote works on philology, mysticism, and other subjects. In 1489, Pico della Mirandola completed his *Heptaplus*, a mystical account of the creation of the universe. His library was one of the largest and most comprehensive of his time. Gave away all his possessions and became a wandering preacher.

1688—1744

POPE, ALEXANDER

English poet and satirist of the English Augustan period who modeled himself after great poets of classical antiquity. Was the foremost poet of his age. He is best known for his poems. Some of his greatest literary works are *An Essay on Criticism*, *The Rape of the Lock*, *The Dunciad*, and *An Essay on Man*, which is believed to be a classic of English neoclassic poetry.

1858—1924

PUCCINI, GIACOMO

Italian operatic composer. Wrote several very successful operas that are often played in opera houses around the world. His most loved operas are *Manon Lescaut*, *La Bohème*, *Tosca*, *Madame Butterfly*, *The Girl of the Golden West*, and *Turandot*. With Verdi and Rossini, he is considered to be one of Italy's greatest operatic composers.

PURCELL, HENRY

England's greatest native composer who wrote virtually all kinds of music known during the restoration. Composed much official and church music. His greatest accomplishments lay in theater music. His masterpiece is *Dido and Aeneas*. He also composed five operas, incidental music to forty-two plays, sonatas, and about one hundred songs.

1658?—1695

PUSHKIN, ALEXANDER SERGEEVICH

Russia's greatest poet. He was the founder of modern Russian literature. Wrote exceptional epic and lyric poems, plays, novels, and short stories. Exerted a profound impact on Russian operatic composers, who based several of their operas on his works. Some of his major works are *The Queen of Spades*, *Eugene Onegin*, and *The Captain's Daughter*.

1799—1837

RABELAIS, FRANÇOIS

French writer, scholar, physician, and humanist. Mostly known for authoring the comic and satirical masterpieces *Pantagruel* and *Gargantua*. His work emphasized individual liberty and excitement for knowledge and life. He is an energetic representative of Renaissance humanism. Had a great influence on Voltaire, Balzac, Swift, and Kingsley.

c1490—1553

RACHMANINOFF, SERGEI WASSILIEVITCH

Russian-American composer, pianist, and conductor. Considered to have been one of the most brilliant pianists of the twentieth century. Rachmaninoff left Russia in 1917 and settled in the United States the following year. His compositions include three symphonies, four piano concertos, the *Rapsody on a Theme by Paganini*, and the choral symphony.

1873—1943

RENOIR, PIERRE AUGUSTE

French painter. Considered to be one of the greatest painters of the Impressionist period. He is noted for his brilliant colors and the charm of his human subjects. In the mid 1880s broke away from the movement to a more formal style. Some of his greatest works are *Le Bal au Moulin de la Galette, Madame Charpentier and Her Children, Woman with Fan,* and *The Swing*. His art is greatly appreciated worldwide and is found in all great museums.

1841—1919

RILKE, RAINER MARIA

Austro-German poet and novelist who wrote mystical, symbolic, impressionistic, and lyrical poetry. His works include *The Book of Hours, The Tale of the Love,* and *Death of Cornet Cristopher Rilke*. Also wrote his famous *Eulogies and Sonnets to Orpheus*. He is regarded as one of the most important and influential modern poets.

1875—1926

1830—1894

ROSSETTI, CHRISTINA GEORGINA

English poet and writer who excelled in poems of fantasy, verse for children, and religious poetry, homilies, and discourses. Considered to be one of the world's greatest female poets. Her major works are *Goblin Market and Other Poems* and *Verses and New Poems*. Also wrote "When I'm Dead, My Dearest," "Uphill," and "A Birthday."

1712—1778

ROUSSEAU, JEAN JACQUES

French philosopher, writer, political theorist, musician, botanist, and one of the most capable writers of the Age of Enlightenment. He inspired the romantic generation and offered ideas on how to minimize social inequality. Was propelled to fame by the essay "Discourse on the Sciences and the Arts," written for the Academie De Dijon. Other major works are *The New Eloise* and *The Social Contract*.

1577—1640

RUBENS, PETER PAUL

Flemish painter considered to be the greatest and most influential of the Flemish masters and one of the most important artists of the seventeenth century. Known for his vibrant, vigorous style and his luminous colors. Several of his paintings are in the Louvre museum in Paris and in other major museums worldwide. Some of his greatest works are *The Raising of the Cross*, *The Descent from the Cross*, and *The Assumption of the Virgin*. Influenced other great artists such as Watteau and Delacroix.

1564–1616

SHAKESPEARE, WILLIAM

English poet, dramatist, and actor often called the English national poet and considered by many to be the greatest dramatist of all time. Some of his greatest comedies are *Comedy of Errors*, *Two Gentlemen of Verona*, and *The Taming of the Shrew*. Also wrote great tragedies such as *Othello*, *Romeo and Juliet*, *Macbeth*, *Hamlet*, and *King Lear*. Because of his great plays and his exquisite sonnets, he is now recognized as one of the world's greatest literary giants.

1856–1950

SHAW, GEORGE BERNARD

Irish comic dramatist and literary critic. Considered to be one of the most important British dramatists since Shakespeare. Some of his works are *The Apple Cart*, *Caesar and Cleopatra*, and *St. Joan*, for which he received the Nobel Prize for literature in 1925. Was a significant influence on his and later generations.

1918–

SOLZHENITSYN, ALEXANDER

Soviet novelist and historian. Imprisoned for criticizing the Soviet regime. Exiled to Central Russia, he taught mathematics and wrote *One Day in the Life of Ivan Denisovich*. Later he wrote his major works: *The Gulag Archipelago*, *The Oak and the Calf*, and *The Mortal Danger*. Considered to be the most important Russian literary artist of the second half of the twentieth century. Was awarded the Nobel Prize for literature in 1970.

SPINOZA, BENEDICT DE

Dutch rationalist philosopher and religious thinker of Portuguese-Jewish descent. Believed to be one of the world's greatest philosophers. His ideas appear in *Ethica* and *Tractatus Teologico-Politicus*. His *Ethica Ordine Geometrico Demonstrata* captures best the essence of his thought. Influenced Leibniz and German idealism.

1632—1677

STOWE, HARRIET BEECHER

American writer and philanthropist. Authored *Uncle Tom's Cabin*, a book that contributed to popular feelings against slavery and the ensuing Civil War. Wrote many studies of social life and published religious poems. Some of her other works are *The Mayflower, Dred: A Tale of the Great Dismal Swamp*, many studies of social life in both fiction and essay, and religious poems.

1811—1896

STRAVINSKY, IGOR FËDOROVICH

Russian-American composer and one of the most influential musical composers of the twentieth century. Had a significant influence on contemporary music. Composed the masterpiece *The Firebird Ballet* and the revolutionary *Le Sacre du Printemps*. Also created neoclassical piano and violin concertos and the Mozartian opera *The Rake's Progress*.

1882—1971

SWIFT, JONATHAN

Anglo-Irish satirist and political journalist. Considered one of the greatest masters of English prose and one of the most effective satirist of his time. Known mostly for his brilliant satire *Gulliver's Travels*, which became a classic story for children. Some of his other major works are *A Modest Proposal* and *Tale of the Tub*.

1667—1745

TASSO, TORQUATO

Italian poet. Considered the most influential poet of the Italian Renaissance. His work includes the beautiful pastoral play *Aminta*, the tragedy *Re Torrismondo*, the epic poem *Rinaldo*, and his immortal epic *Jerusalem Delivered*. He was summoned to Rome to be crowned poet laureate but died before the ceremony could take place.

1544—1595

TCHAIKOVSKY, PETER ILYICH

Russian composer. Considered to be a master melodist. He composed several outstanding works, among which are the *Symphonie Pathetique*, the operas *Eugene Onegin* and *Pique Dance*, the ballets *Swan Lake* and *Sleeping Beauty*, and his world-renowned *Nutcracker Suite*.

1840—1893

TENNYSON, ALFRED

English poet, often regarded as the chief representative of the Victorian age in poetry. His first work, *Poems Chiefly Lyrical*, appeared while he was still a student at Cambridge. Some of his works are *The Princess, In Memoriam, The Charge of the Light Brigade,* and *Ballads and Other Poems.* Also wrote several plays. He was raised to peerage in 1884.

1809—1892

THOREAU, HENRY DAVID

American essayist and naturalist. Lover of the simple life. Lived in a cabin at Walden Pond for two years and, as a result, wrote the classic *Walden, or Life in the Woods.* Was a strong antislavery man and an energetic Transcendentalist. His fame grew after his death. Also wrote *The Maine Woods, Excursions,* and *Cape Cod.*

1817—1862

TOLSTOY, LEO

Russian novelist and philosopher. Wrote two of the greatest of all novels: *War and Peace* and *Anna Karenina.* His conversion to religion is described in his *Confessions.* By the time of his death he had given away all of his possessions to the poor and needy. He was devoted to social reform. Also wrote *Resurrection* and *The Power of Darkness.*

1828—1910

1694—1778

VOLTAIRE

French author, playwright, philosopher, and one of the greatest authors of the eighteenth century. A crusader against tyranny and bigotry. Noted for his satire and critical ability. His best-known plays are *Zaire, Merope,* and *Mohamet.* His satirical stories, *Candide* and *Zadig,* and his long epic *La Henriade* are also famous.

1909—1943

WEIL, SIMONE

French mystic social philosopher whose works had particular influence on French and English social thought. Wrote *Cahiers du Sud, La Pesanteur et la Grace, Waiting for God, The Need for Roots,* and *Fully Dedicated to God and Christ.*

1889—1951

WITTGENSTEIN, LUDWIG

Austrian-born English philosopher who was one of the most influential figures in British philosophy during the second quarter of the twentieth century. Produced two original and influential systems of philosophical thought: logical theories and philosophy of language. Wrote the *Tractatus Logico-Philosophicus* and *Philosophical Investigations.*

1770—1850

WORDSWORTH, WILLIAM

Major English Romantic poet and poet laureate of England. His *Lyrical Ballads*, written with Samuel Taylor Coleridge, helped launch the English Romantic Movement. Also wrote *The Prelude*, very fine lyrics, and *The Excursion*. His theories and style contributed to a new tradition in poetry.

SOURCES

Drimmer, H. *The New University One Volume Encyclopaedia*. New York: New University Encyclopaedia Division, 1967.
Encyclopaedia Britannica. Toronto: Encyclopaedia Britannica, Inc., 1989.
Microsoft Encarta Encyclopaedia 99. Microsoft Corporation.

INTRODUCTION

1. Kierkegaard, S. *Sören Kierkegaard—Journal and Papers*, Vol. II, F–K. London: Indiana University Press, 1970, 93.
2. Auden, W. H. *The Living Thoughts of Kierkegaard*. London: Indiana University Press, London, 1966, 143.
3. Christiansen, G. E. *In the Presence of the Creator*. New York: The Free Press, 1984, 257.
4. Burgelin, P. *La Philosophie de l'Existence de Jean Jacques Rousseau*. Librarie Philosophique J. Vrin, 1973, 414.
5. Emerson, R. W. *The Complete Prose Works*. London: Ward, Lock and Co. Ltd. 1900, 74.
6. Pinney, T. *Essays of George Eliot*. New York: Columbia University Press, 1963, 242–43.
7. Rewald, J. *Paul Cézanne*. London: Westbook House, 1950, 101.
8. "Robert Browning." *Encyclopedia Britannica*. 15th Edition. Chicago: Encyclopedia Britannica, Inc., 1974, 336.
9. Delacroix, E. *Journal de Eugène Delacroix*. Librarie Plon, 1932, 697.
10. La Mara. *Letters of Franz Liszt*. New York: Haskell House Publishers, 1968, 544.
11. Tolstoy, L. *Patriotism Slavery of Our Times*. New York: Thomas Y. Crowell Co. Publishers, 1927, 308.
12. Leaver, R. J. S. *Bach and Scripture*. St. Louis: Concordia Publishing House, 1985, 29.
13. Clarck, R. *The Life and Times of Einstein*. New York: The World Publishing Co., 1971, 18–19.
14. Leaver, R. J. S. *Bach and Scripture*, 13.
15. Kalischer, A. C. *Beethoven's Letters*. New York: J. M. Dent and Co., 1926, 391.
16. Goethe, J. *The Autobiography of Goethe Vol. 1*. New York: John D. Williams, 1882, 208.
17. Beer, A. *Kepler—Four Hundred Years*. Oxford: Pergamom Press, 1975, 356.
18. Rosemberg, J. *Rembrandt, Life and Work*. London: Phaidon Press, 1964, 181.

19. Tolstoy, L. *My Confessions, My Religion. The Gospel in Brief.* New York: Charles Scribners and Sons, 1899.
20. Alighieri, D. *On World Government.* The Library of Liberal Arts, 1957, II, vii.
21. Schubert, F. *Franz Schubert's Letters and Other Writings.* Westport, Conn.: Greenwood Press, 1970, 115.
22. Rowse, A. L. *Shakespeare's Self-Portrait.* University Press of America, 1985, 182.
23. Wittgenstein, L. *Notebooks—1914–1916.* Oxford: University of Chicago Press, 1979, 4–5.
24. Bacon, F. *The Essays of Lord Bacon.* London: Longman and Green Co., 1875, 64.

GREAT ARTISTS

BLAKE, WILLIAM
"It is God" (Keynes, G. *The Poetry and Prose of William Blake, Vol. I.* London: The Nonesuch Library, 1961, 733).
"Come, o Thou Lamb" (Ibid., 497).
"If God is anything" (Ibid., 733).
"God is in the lowest" (Ibid., 733).
"Man must have" (Ibid., 498).

BUONARROTI, MICHELANGELO
"My dear Lord" (Stone, I., Stone, J., Speroni, C. *Michelangelo Buonarroti, Lettere.* Milano: Dall'oglio, Editore, 1963, 245).
"Unless Thou show" (Wordsworth,W. *The Complete Poetical Works.* Cambridge: Riverside Press, 1932, 319).
"Only You are" (D'Angelo, P. *La Poesia Di Michelangelo.* Herbita Editrice, 1978, 127).
"Do not look" (Ibid., 127).
"I would love" (Ibid., 78).
"The vanities of life" (Ibid., 133).
"By the cross" (Ibid., 131).

CÉZANNE, PAUL
"I am helpless" (Mack, G. *Paul Cézanne.* London: Jonathan Cape, 1935, 281).

"Let me repeat" (Ibid., 377–78).
"Once we have attained" (Rewald, J. *Paul Cézanne*. London: Westbook House, 1950).

DA VINCI, LEONARDO
"I obey Thee" (Richter, J. *The Literary Works of Leonardo da Vinci, Vol. II*. Phaidon Press, 1970, 237).
"A lie is" (Ibid., 242).
"You think that" (Ibid., 238).
"The works of God" (Ibid., 387).

DELACROIX, EUGÈNE
"Does nature promise" (Delacroix, E. *Selected Letters, 1813–1863*. Translated by Jean Stuart. London: Eyre and Spittiswoode, 1971, 229).
"God is within" (Delacroix, E. *Journal de Eugène Delacroix*. Librairie Plon, 1932, 329).

DÜRER, ALBRECHT
"And if here below" (Conway, Lord, *The Literary Remains of Albrecht Dürer*. New York: Cambridge University Press, 1889, 93).
"Oh highest heavenly Father" (Ibid., 91).

INGRES, JEAN AUGUSTE DOMINIQUE
"If God allows me" (Ingres, J. A. D. *Pensèes et Ècrits du Peintre*. Geneve: Pierre Cailler, Editor, 1947, 40).
"May God preserve" (Ibid., 123).
"Have religion" (Ibid., 45).

RENOIR, PIERRE AUGUSTE
"I believe, therefore" (Weaver, R. *Renoir, My Father*. London: Collins, 1962, 218).
"I believe that" (Ibid., 218).

RUBENS, PETER PAUL
"I pray to God" (Rubens, P. *The Letters of Peter Paul Rubens*. Cambridge: Harvard University Press, 1955, 202).
"I can finish" (Ibid., 99).

"I call the Lord" (Ibid., 96).
"It rests upon" (Ibid., 145).
"I pray also" (Ibid., 246).
"I know of nothing" (Ibid., 203).

GREAT MUSICIANS

BACH, JOHANN SEBASTIAN
"God, who sees" (Terry, C. *Bach*. London: Oxford U. Press, 1967, 246. Used by permission of Oxford University Press).
"God prescribes" (Ibid., 114).
"I can only bear" (Ibid., 245).
"God is" (Ibid., 113).
"To the Highest" (Leaver, R. *J. S. Bach and Scripture*. St. Louis: Concordia Publishing House, 1985, 29).

BEETHOVEN, LUDWIG VAN
"God is immaterial" (Kalischer, A. C. *Beethoven's Letters*. New York: J. M. Dent and Co., 1926, 393–94).

GLUCK, CHRISTOPH WILLIBALD VON
"I commend my soul" (Mueller Von Asow, H., Mueller Von Asow, E. *The Collected Correspondence and Papers of Cristoph Willebrand Gluck*. London: Barrie and Rockcliff, 1962, 174).
"I thank God" (Ibid., 206).

HANDEL, GEORGE FRIDERIC
"Ye servants of th'eternal King" (Burrows, D. *Handel*. New York: Oxford University Press, 1994, 320. Used by permission of Oxford University Press).
"Oh first created" (Ibid., 321).

HAYDN, FRANZ JOSEPH
"May the Almighty" (Robbins Landon, H. C. *Haydn—A Documented Study*. New York: Rizzoli, 1981, 241).
"The Emperor Franz" (Ibid., 187).
"I thank my Creator" (Ibid., 120).

"The Almighty" (Ibid.).

"Never before" (Butterworth, N. *Haydn—His Life and Times*. Chapel River Press, 1977, 122).

LISZT, FRANZ

"Everything is transitory" (Walker, A. *Franz Liszt*. New York: Cornell University Press, 1989, 544).

"Yes 'Jesus Christ on the cross'" (La Mara. *Letters of Franz Liszt*. New York: Haskell House Publishers, 1968, 439).

MASCAGNI, PIETRO

"We Christians know" (Morini, M. *Pietro Mascagni*. Milano: Casa Musicale Sanzogno di Piero Ostali, 1964, 180).

"I have absolute faith" (Ibid.).

"Jesus was Divinity" (Ibid., 175).

"Art, to be truly art" (Ibid.).

MOZART, WOLFGANG AMADEUS

"Let us trust" (Mersmann, H. *Letters of Mozart*. London: J. M. Dent and Sons, 1938, 106).

"No physician" (Ibid.).

"God, who ordains all" (Ibid., 105–6).

"Let us submit" (Ibid., 108).

PUCCINI, GIACOMO

"So far, God" (Adani, G. *Letters of Puccini*. New York: AMS Press, 1971, 111).

"I was born" (Ibid., 179).

"May it be" (Ibid., 196).

"I don't say" (Ibid., 296).

PURCELL, HENRY

"It is not fit" (Zimmermann, F. B. *Henry Purcell—1659–1695—His Life and Times*. New York: Saint Martin's Press, 1967, 30. Used by permission of The Humanities Press).

"My soul I surrender" (Ibid., 368).

RACHMANINOFF, SERGEI WASSILIEVITCH

"No prophet I" (Von Resmann, O. *Rachmaninoff's Recollections*. New York: Books for Libraries Press, 1970, 225).

"Blessed art Thou" (Martin, B. *Rachmaninoff, Composer, Pianist, Conductor*. Aldershot, Hans, England: Scolar Press, 1990, 257).

STRAVINSKY, IGOR FËDOROVICH
"My artistic goal" (Stravinsky, V., Craft, R. *Stravinsky in Pictures and Documents*. New York: Simon and Schuster, 1978, 552. Copyright by Vera Stravinsky, Trapezoid Inc., and Robert Craft).
"The more one separates" (Ibid., 295).

TCHAIKOVSKY, PETER ILYICH
"The night" (Tchaikovsky, M. *The Life and Letters of Peter Tchaikovsky*. New York: Haskell House Publishers, 1970, 381).
"For some time" (Ibid., 500).
"Whenever I think" (Ibid., 228).
"God give you" (Ibid., 450).
"[Christ] who prayed" (Ibid., 504).

GREAT PHILOSOPHERS

BACON, FRANCIS
"God has this attribute" (Bacon, F. *The Essays of Lord Bacon*. London: Longman and Green Co., 1875, 10).
"They that deny" (Ibid., 67).
"It were better" (Ibid., 68).
"It is true" (Ibid., 64).

BRUNO, GIORDANO
"The Universal Intellect" (Giordano, B. *Cause, Principle and Unity*. Background Books, 1962, 81).
"Cause, Principle, Eternal Unity" (Ibid., 55).

CAMPANELLA, TOMMASO
"It is up" (Tuscano, P. *Poetica e Poesia di Tommaso Campanella*. Edizioni I. P. L. 1969, 135–36).
"He who rises" (Ibid., 120).
"I believe in God" (Ibid., 160).
"I come to Thee" (Ibid., 141).

"Think, oh man" (Guzzo, A., Amerio, R. *Opere di Giordano Bruno e di Tommaso Campanella*. Milano: Riccardo Ricciardi Editore, 1966, 922, 924).

DESCARTES, RENÉ
"By the name" (Descartes, R. "Les Meditations" in *The Meditations and Selections from the Principles of René Descartes*. La Salle, Ill.: Open Court Publ. Co., 1950, Par. 155).
"The idea of" (Ibid., Par. 177).
"I have concluded" (Ibid.).
"In God we encounter" (Ibid., Par. 158).
"It is quite evident" (Ibid., Par. 176).
"It is sufficient" (Ibid., Par. 2).
"It is absolutely" (Ibid.).
"I conceive of God" (Ibid., Par. 160).

FICHTE, JOHANN GOTTLIEB
"Nothing exists outside" (Bliss-Talbot, E. *The Fundamental Principles of Fichte's Philosophy*. New York: The Macmillan Company, 1906, 72).
"What is outside" (Ibid.).
"For freedom is always" (Ibid., 100).
"God Himself" (Ibid.).
"In the beginning" (Ibid.).
"God is pure" (Ibid., 74).
"One thinks of God" (Ibid., 114).
"My scheming spirit" (Adamson, R., *Fichte*. London: William Blackwood and Sons, 1881, 21).

HEGEL, GEORG WILHELM FRIEDRICH
"God is Spirit" (Hegel, G. W. F. *Lectures on the Philosophy of Religion*, *Vol. I*. Kegan, Paul, Trench, Trubner and Co. Ltd., 1895, 92).
"God in His universality" (Ibid.).
"God is the One" (Ibid., 99).
"God is good" (Ibid.).
"All is God" (Ibid., 96).
"To think of God" (Ibid., 95).

"God is the beginning" (Ibid., 2).
"In God" (Ibid., 98).

JAMES, WILLIAM
"I do not know" (James, W. *The Will to Believe and Other Essays in Popular Psychology*. New York: Longmans Green and Co., 1907, 61).

KANT, IMMANUEL
"The sum total" (Kant, I. *Lectures on Philosophical Theology*. Ithaca: Cornell University Press, 1978, 23. Used by permission of the publisher, Cornell University Press).
"God's omnipresence is" (Ibid., 151).
"God has no need" (Ibid., 153).
"God is the only" (Ibid., 156).
"God created the world" (Ibid., 142–43).
"Morality leads" (Kant, I. *Oeuvres Philosophiques*. Editions Gallimard, 1986, 18–19).
"The true (moral) worship" (Ibid., 231).

KIERKEGAARD, SÖREN
"All other religions" (Wahl, J. *Ètude Kierkegaardiennes*. Paris: Librarie Philosophique, J. Vrin, 1967, 516).
"What is special" (Ibid., 543).
"I have a child-father" (Ibid.).
"God is infinitely" (Ibid., 567).
"If I am" (Ibid., 564).
"I am seeing" (Ibid.).
"God is infinite" (Ibid., 544).
"When Christ cried" (Ibid., 565).
"He who sees" (Ibid.).
"Worldly wisdom teaches" (Ibid., 604).
"Christianity teaches categorically" (Masi, G. *Disperazione e Speranza*. Padova: Editrice Gregoriana, 1971, 186).
"He who is" (Ibid.).
"For as long" (Ibid., 188).
"In loving God" (Ibid., 190).

LEIBNIZ, GOTTFRIED WILHELM VON

"For what greater" (Loemker, L. E. *Philosophical Papers and Letters*. Boston: D. Reidel Publishing Co., 1976, 280).

"Power and knowledge" (Ibid., 304).

"With absolute certainty" (Nourisson, M. *La Philosophie De Leibniz*. Paris: Librarie De L. hachette et Cle, 1860, 359).

"Let's consider God" (Ibid.).

"God...has no" (Ibid., 308).

"I have always" (Ibid., 356).

"When we separate" (Ibid., 311).

"If the smallest" (Olgiati, F. *Il Significato Storico di Leibniz*. Milano: Societá Editrice Vita e Pensiero, 1929, 201).

"No sleep may" (Ibid., 181).

"God, who is" (Ibid., 182).

"I find God" (Ibid., 37).

"Wise and virtuous" (Ibid., 200).

MILL, JOHN STUART

"I think it" (Mill, J. *Essays on Ethics, Religion, and Society*. Toronto: University of Toronto Press, 1969, 450).

"Among the facts" (Ibid., 439).

"In voluntary action" (Ibid., 437).

PASCAL, BLAISE

"Let man reverting" (Pascal, B. *Thoughts on Religion and Philosophy*. Edimburgh: Otto Schultz and Co., 2–3).

"All things have" (Ibid., 5).

"Every thing in the world" (Ibid., 134).

"Instead of complaining" (Ibid., 137).

"The stoics said" (Ibid., 11–12).

"It is invariably" (Ibid., 133).

"I perceive it" (Ibid., 13).

PICO DELLA MIRANDOLA, GIOVANNI

"We conceive God" (Pico della Mirandola. *On the Dignity of Man*. New York: The Bobbs-Merrill Co., Inc., 1940, 59).

"God is most" (Ibid.).

"God is the fullest" (Ibid., 60)

"God is infinite" (Ibid., 48)

"God is being" (Ibid., 49)

"Now the highest" (Ibid., 4).

ROUSSEAU, JEAN JACQUES

"If God exists" (Guehenno, J. *Jean Jacques Rousseau*. New York: Columbia University Press, 1966, 350. Reprinted by permission of the publisher).

"Forgive me, great man" (Ibid., 351).

"(The Bible) is" (Burgelin, P. *La Philosophie de l'Existance de Jean Jacques Rousseau*. Librarie Philosophique J. Vrin, 1973, 429).

"I will never" (Ibid., 407).

"An intelligent being" (Ibid.).

"The blackboard of nature" (Ibid., 414).

"Worship the Eternal" (Ibid., 419).

"No, God of my soul" (Ibid., 415).

SPINOZA, BENEDICT DE

"We cannot be" (Elwes, R. H. M. *The Chief Works of Benedict de Spinoza, Vol. II*. New York: Dover Publications, Inc., 1951, 53. Used by permission of Dover Publications).

"Without God" (Ibid., 60).

"God and His attributes are unchangeable" (Ibid., 63).

"God and His attributes are eternal" (Ibid.).

"Besides God" (Ibid., 55).

"Things have been" (Ibid., 71).

"Wherefore the omnipotence" (Ibid., 61).

VOLTAIRE

"All nature" (Parton, J. *Life of Voltaire, Vol. II*. Boston: Houghton, Mofflin and Co., 1884, 554).

"If God did not exist, it" (Ibid.).
"I die, adoring God" (Ibid., 577).
"What is true" (Pomeau, R. *Ecraser L'Infame, 1759–1770*. Voltaire Foundation, 1995, 386).
"We want a religion" (Ibid., 338).
"Let's worship" (Ibid., 339).
"[God] is the supreme being" (Ibid., 385).
"If God did not exist, everything" (Ibid., 660).
"Praying means submitting" (Ibid., 662).
"[God is] supreme" (Ibid.).
"Christ consoles" (Ibid., 661).
"Tonight I was" (Redman, B. R. *The Portable Voltaire*. New York: Viking Press, 1863, 187).

WEIL, SIMONE
"One must feel" (Davy, M. *The Mysticism of Simone Weil*. London: Rockcliffe, Salysbury Sq, 1951, 33).
"Christ descended" (Ibid., 34).
"It is in affliction" (Panichas, G. A. *The Simone Weil Reader*. New York: David McKay Co., Inc.,
    1977, 107).
"I was brought" (Ibid., 111).
"Christ…is" (Ibid., 23).
"Every existing thing" (Ibid., 113).
"I do not" (Ibid., 106).
"The cross is" (Perrin, M., Thibon, G. *Simone Weil telle que nous l'avons connue*. Paris: Librarie
    Artheme, 1967, 39).
"God is absolute" (Ibid.).
"God has created" (Ibid., 38).
"I am as totally" (Ibid., 47).
"We should give" (Weil, S. *The Notebooks of Simone Weil, Vol. I*. London: Routledge and Kegan
    Publishing, 1956, 326).
"If we really" (Ibid., 322).

WITTGENSTEIN, LUDWIG
"Certainly it is" (Wittgenstein, L. *Notebooks—1914–1916*. Oxford: University of Chicago Press,
    1979, 75E).

"How things stand" (Ibid., 79E).

"What we are dependent" (Ibid., 74E).

"The meaning of life" (Brand, G. *The Central Texts of Ludwig Wittgenstein*. Oxford: Basil Blackwell, 1979, 165).

"To pray is" (Ibid.).

"The good is" (Ibid., 164).

GREAT SCIENTISTS

BRAHE, TYCHO

"God...from whom" (Brahe, T. *The English Experience*. New York: Da Capo Press, 1969, 1).

"It is impossible" (Ibid., 20).

"God who ruleth" (Ibid., 19).

COPERNICUS, NICOLAUS

"God, without whom" (Copernicus, N. *On the Revolutions of the Celestial Spheres*. Thorn: Societas Copernicana, 1873, 12).

"For who, after applying" (Ibid., 510–11).

EINSTEIN, ALBERT

"I defend the" (Speziali, P. *Albert Einstein–Michele Basso Correspondence, 1903–1955*. Paris: Herman, 1972, 425).

"You believe in" (Schilpp, P. A. *Albert Einstein, Philosopher-Scientist*. London: Cambridge University Press, 1969, 176. Reprinted with the permission of Cambridge University Press).

"I believe in" (Ibid., 103).

"I'm not much" (Clarck, R. *The Life and Times of Einstein*. New York: The World Publishing Co., 1971, 18–19).

"The scientist's religious" (Iain, P. *Science, Theology and Einstein*. New York: Oxford University Press, 1982, 57).

FARADAY, MICHAEL

"And though the" (Jones, B. *The Life and Letters of Faraday, Vol. II*. London: Longmans, Green, and Co., 1870, 424).

"Though we may" (Ibid., 425).

"The Christian…is" (Ibid., 426).

"I bow before" (Ibid., 471).

"I am content" (Jones, B. *The Life and Letters of Faraday, Vol. I*. London: Longmans, Green, and Co., 1870, 298–99).

GALILEI, GALILEO

"May it be" (Poupard, Cardinal Paul. *Galileo Galilei*. Pittsburgh: Duquesne University Press, 1983, 42. Used by permission of Duquesne University Press).

"When I reflect" (Ibid., 101).

"God could have" (Ibid., 99).

"One must not" (Brunetti, F. *Opere di Galileo Galilei, Vol. II*. 1964, 545).

"I trust the infinite" (Ibid., 550).

"To the Lord" (Chiari, A. *Galileo Galilei, Scritti Letterari*. Florence: Felice Le Monnier, 1970, 321).

HARVEY, WILLIAM

"We acknowledge God" (Harvey, W. *Anatomical Exercises on the Generation of Animals*. Toronto: Great Books of the Western World, William Benton, Publisher, Vol. 28, 443).

"The Omnipotent Maker" (Keynes, G. *The Life of William Harvey*. Oxford: Oxford University Press, 1978, 94. Used by permission of Oxford University Press).

"The examination of" (Ibid., 330).

KEPLER, JOHANN

"Geometry…coeternal" (Beer, A. *Kepler—Four Hundred Years*. Oxford: Pergamom Press, 1975, 75).

"But we Christians" (Ibid., 356).

"Great is our Lord" (Ibid., 361).

NEWTON, SIR ISAAC

"The supreme God" (Thayer, H. S. *Newton's Philosophy of Nature*. New York: Hafner Publishing Company, 1953, 45).

"As a blind man" (Ibid.).

"From His true dominion" (Burtt, E. A. *The Methaphysical Foundations of Modern Science*. New York: The Humanities Press, Inc., 1951, 257).

"He endureth forever" (Ibid.).

Pasteur, Louis

"In good philosophy" (Geison, G. L. *The Private Science of Louis Pasteur*. Princeton: Princeton University Press, 1995, 141–42. Used by permission of Princeton University Press).

"The atmosphere in" (Cuny, H. *Louis Pasteur, The Man and His Theories*. New York: Paul S. Eriksson, Inc., 1966, 161).

GREAT WRITERS

Alighieri, Dante

"We should know" (Alighieri, D. *On World Government*. The Library of Liberal Arts, 1957, I, iii).

"Mankind is best" (Ibid., ix).

"Christ…is the door" (Ibid., II, vii).

"Whatever in human" (Ibid., ii).

"God alone elevates" (Ibid., III, viii).

"The glory of Him" (Alighieri, D. *Paradiso*. http://italian.about.com/homework/italian/library/anthology/dante/blparadisoindex.htm, I, 1–3).

"I believe in" (Ibid., XXIV, 125–32).

Brontë, Emily

"No coward soul" (Brontë, E. "No Coward Soul Is Mine." http://www.library.utoronto.ca/utel/rp/poems/brontee3c.html, 1998).

"The world is" (Inge, W. R. *God and the Astronomers*. Toronto: Longmans, Green, and Co., 1933, 16).

Browning, Elizabeth Barrett

"So oft the doing" (Ricks, R. *The Brownings: Letters and Poetry*. New York: Doubleday and Co., 1970, 134).

"God hath transfixed" (Ibid., 138).

"God keeps His" (Ibid., 165).

"God is the perfect" (Ibid., 28).

"God the creator" (Ibid., 136–37).

Browning, Robert

"From the heart" (Browning, R. *The Works of Robert Browning*. London: Smith, Elder and Co., 1912, 11–42).

"How very hard" (Ibid., 44).
"Thou Love of God!" (Ibid., 74).

CHAUCER, GEOFFREY
"I thank the Lord" (Howard, D. R. *Chaucer, His Life, His Works, His World*. New York: A William Abrahams Book, 1987, 500).
"Now pray them" (Ibid., 499–500).

CHEKHOV, ANTON PAVLOVICH
"One should believe" (Hellman, L. *The Selected Letters of Anton Checkov*. McGraw-Hill Book Co., 1955, 286).
"Present-day culture" (Heim, M. H. *Letters of Anton Checkov*. New York: Harper and Rowe, 1973, 436).

DEFOE, DANIEL
"To say it" (Defoe, D. *The Novels and Miscellaneous Works of Daniel De Foe, Vol. 13*. London: D. A. Talboys, 1840, 56).
"God…has posted" (Ibid., 56–57).

DELEDDA, GRAZIA
"I love my" (Scano, A. *Grazia Deledda, Versi e Prose Giovanili*. Milano: Edizioni Virgilio, 1972, 38).
"I see my future" (Deledda, G. *Opere Scelte*. Milano: Arnoldo Mondadori Editore, 1964, 1106).

DICKENS, CHARLES
"I now most" (Walder, D. *Dickens and Religion*. London: George Allen and Unwin, 1981, 195).
"I have always" (Ibid.).
"Remember! It is Christianity" (Ibid., 13).
"The Divine teacher" (Ibid., 175).
"Nothing is discovered" (Ibid.).

DONNE, JOHN
"Thou has made me" (Donne, J. *The Complete Poetry and Selected Prose*. New York: The Modern Library, 236).
"As due by many" (Ibid.).
"But who am I" (Ibid., 239).
"For, if we consider" (Ibid., 350–51).

DOSTOEVSKY, FYODOR MIKHAILOVICH
"I have often" (Lowe, D. A. *Fyodor Dostoevsky, Complete Letters, Volume Five, 1878–1881*. Ann Arbor: Ardis, 1991, 290).
"People here are trying" (Ibid., 302).
"I place my trust" (Lloyd, J. A. T. *Fyodor Dostoevsky*. London: Eyre and Spottiswoode, 1947, 191).
"My hour has come" (Ibid., 199).

DRYDEN, JOHN
"What weight of ancient witness" (Untermyer, L. *Lives of the Poets*. New York: Simon and Schuster, 1959, 205).

ELIOT, T. S.
"We build in vain" (Buxton, E. W. *Creative Living...Five*. Toronto: W. J. Gage and Co., 520).
"O weariness of men" (Ibid., 520–21).
"Lord, shall we" (Smidt, K. *Poetry and Belief in the Work of T. S. Eliot*. New York: Humanities Press, 1961, 55).

EMERSON, RALPH WALDO
"It now shows" (Emerson, R. W. *The Complete Prose Works*. London: Ward, Lock and Co., Ltd., 1900, 77).
"How dear, how soothing" (Ibid., 74).
"If he [man]" (Ibid.).
"In God every" (Ibid., 319).
"Our globe seen" (Ibid., 75).
"As a plant" (Ibid., 325).
"The ardors of piety" (Hayford, H. *Classic American Writers*. Toronto: Little, Brown and Co., 1962, 87).

FRANKLIN, BENJAMIN
"Here is my creed" (Franklin, B. *Benjamin Franklin's Autobiography*. New York: Rinehart and Co., Inc., 1959, 292).
"And conceiving God" (Ibid., 88).

GOETHE, JOHANN WOLFGANG VON
"General, natural religion" (Goethe, J. *The Autobiography of Goethe Vol. 1*. New York: John D. Williams, 1882, 114).
"English, French, and Germans" (Ibid., 227).

GOGOL, NIKOLAI VASILIEVICH
"The Christian will" (Zeldin, J. *Selected Passages from Correspondence with Friends, by Nikolai Gogol*. Nashville: Vanderbilt University Press, 1969, 82).
"Leaf through the Old Testament" (Ibid., 86).
"The higher truths" (Ibid., 23).
"Great is the God" (Ibid., 90).
"All the gifts" (Ibid., 91).
"Go on your knees" (Ibid., 88).

HEINE, HEINRICH
"Faulting the Creator's" (Draper, H. *The Complete Poems of Heinrich Heine*. Boston: Suhrkamp / Insel, 1982, 801).
"God has made" (Ibid., 799).
"God's satire weighs" (Pinney, T. *Essays of George Eliot*. New York: Columbia Univ. Press, 1963, 245).

HUGO, VICTOR
"Cathedrals are beautiful" (Hugo, V. *Oeuvres Poètique*. Bibliotheque de la Pleiade, 1967, 565).
"Lord, I suffer" (Ibid., 840).
"My Lord, my whole" (Ibid., 841).
"Let us love!" (Ibid., 566).
"Let us rely" (Hugo, V. *Les Contemplations*. Paris: Editions Garnier Freres, 1969, 345).
"We are darkness" (Ibid.).

KAFKA, FRANZ
"Today the longing" (Janouch, G. *Conversations with Kafka*. Andre Deutch, 1968, 51).

LAMARTINE, ALPHONSE
"I thought I understood" (Lamartine, A. *Poesie Inedites*. Paris: Hachette, Furne, Jouet, 1873, 151).
"Man should serve" (Ibid., 274).

"Providence brings" (Ibid., 150).
"God is, the ultimate" (Ibid., 152).
"All true Christians" (Ibid., 276).

LEOPARDI, GIACOMO
"If God is above" (Leopardi, G. *Opere, Tomo II*. Milano: Riccardo Ricciardi Editore, 1977, 358).
"The ten commandments" (Ibid., 356).
"I consider God" (Ibid., 351).

LONGFELLOW, HENRY WADSWORTH
"Wondrous truths" (Longfellow, H. *The Poetical Works*. London: George Routledge and Sons, 1871, 5).

LOWELL, JAMES RUSSELL
"God! do not let" (Lowell, J. *The Complete Poetical Works*. New York: Houghton, Mifflin and Co., 1895, 15).

MANZONI, ALESSANDRO
"With faithful love" (De Castris, A. *Tutte le Poesie di Alessandro Manzoni*. Florence: Sansoni, 1965, 166).
"You are mine" (Ibid.).
"Look down merciful God" (Ibid., 165).
"Who shaped plants' " (Ibid.).

MAZZINI, GIUSEPPE
"Christianity is a (fixed)" (Griffith, G. *Mazzini: Prophet of Modern Europe*. London: Hodder and Stoughton, 1932, 106).
"I believe in God" (Ibid.).
"Christianity is the formula" (Ibid., 107).
"God is our defence" (Ibid., 115).
"I fear, dear friend" (Ibid., 334).
"Yes! Yes!" (Ibid., 355).
"Above all beliefs" (Ibid., 149).

MELVILLE, HERMAN
"The reason the" (Hayford, H. *Classic American Writers*. Toronto: Little, Brown and Co., 1962, 331).
"We incline to think" (Ibid., 329).

MILTON, JOHN

"We may be sure" (Robins, H. *If This Be Heresy—A Study of Milton and Origen*. Philadelphia: University of Pennsylvania Press, 1963, 67. Used by permission of University of Pennsylvania Press).

"Let us require" (Ibid.).

"If after the work" (Ibid.).

"Thee Father first" (Milton, J. *Paradise Lost, Book III*, 372–82; http://www.shu.ac.uk/emls/iemls/resour/mirrors/eshp/lost/lost.html, 1999).

PENN, WILLIAM

"Country life" (Elliot, C. W. *William Penn—Fruits of Solitude*. New York: P. F. Collier and Sons, 1937, 342).

"As puppets are" (Ibid.).

"Love is above all" (Ibid., 367).

"God's works declare" (Ibid., 366).

"Religion itself" (Ibid.).

"Whatever else" (Ibid., 328).

PETRARCH, FRANCESCO

"Bowing one's knees" (Petrarch, F. *Canzoniere*. Fratelli Fabbri Editori, 1969, 47).

"Heavenly Father" (Neri, F. *Rime e Trionfi di Francesco Petrarca*. Torino: Unione Tipografico-editrice Torinese, 118).

POPE, ALEXANDER

"Is the great chain" (Roscoe, W. *The Works of Alexander Pope*. London: Longman, Brown and Co., 1847, 25).

"God, in the nature" (Ibid., 11).

"That chain that links" (Ibid., 13).

"Say first, of world" (Ibid., 24).

PUSHKIN, ALEXANDER SERGEEVICH

"Pure men and women too" (Yarmolinsky, A. *The Poems, Prose and Plays of Alexander Pushkin*. New York: The Modern Library, 1964, 86).

RABELAIS, FRANÇOIS
"When you say" (Febvre, L. *Le Probleme de l'Incroyance au XVIe Siecle*. Paris: Editions Albin
    Michel, 1962, 262).
"Man must serve" (Ibid., 274).
"Let us pray" (Ibid., 266).
"We are all sinners" (Ibid., 270).
"What takes place" (Ibid., 263).

RILKE, RAINER MARIA
"All love is" (Rilke, R. M. *Selected Letters, 1902–1926*. New York: Quartet Encounter, 1988, 233).
"I know God" (Ibid., 106).
"First you must" (Ibid., 335).

ROSSETTI, CHRISTINA GEORGINA
"Sweet thou art pale" (Rossetti, C. "The Three Enemies." http://www.library.utoronto.ca/utel/rp/
    poems/rossettc4.html, 1998).

SHAKESPEARE, WILLIAM
"Now, God be" (Shakespeare, W. *The Complete Works of Shakespeare*. New York: Nelson Doubleday,
    Inc., II Henry VI, Act ii, sc. 1, 66).
"God's greatness" (Ibid., 85).
"God shall be" (Ibid., sc. 3, 24).
"God, the best maker" (Ibid., Henry V, Act v, sc. 2, 387).
"We are in" (Ibid., Act iii, sc. 6, 178).
"In the name" (Rowse, A. L. *Shakespeare's Self-Portrait*. University Press of America, 1985, 182).

SHAW, GEORGE BERNARD
"O Lord our God" (Shaw, W. S. *Shaw on Religion*. New York: Dodd, Mead, and Company, 1967, 184).
"All life is a series" (Ibid., 129).
"I am ready" (Ibid., 64).
"I believe that" (Ibid., 128).

SOLZHENITSYN, ALEXANDER
"How easy it is" (Burg, D., Feiffer, G. *Solzhenitzyn, A Biography*. Stein and Day, 1972, 189).

STOWE, HARRIET BEECHER

"God always makes" (Wagenknecht, E. *Harriet Beecher Stowe*. New York: Oxford University Press, 1965, 177).

"I think the" (Ibid., 203).

"Still, still with Thee" (Ibid., 211).

"He [Harriet's brother]" (Ibid., 217).

"For who is" (Ibid., 218).

"My God is" (Ibid., 212).

SWIFT, JONATHAN

"God's mercy is" (Eddy, W. A. *Satires and Personal Writings by Jonathan Swift*. London: Oxford University Press, 1932, 418).

"Miserable mortals!" (Ibid., 419).

TASSO, TORQUATO

"Father in heaven" (Tasso, T. *Poesie*. Milano: Riccardo Ricciardi Editore, 1952, 925).

TENNYSON, ALFRED

"Hallowed be Thy name" (Mastermann, C. *Tennyson as a Religious Teacher*. London: Methuen and Co., 1900, 57).

"We feel we" (Ibid.).

"Take away belief" (Ibid., 54).

"If God were" (Ibid., 55).

"When Moses" (Ricks, C. *The Poems of Tennyson*. Longmans, 1969, 1808).

"Fear not" (Ibid., 1456).

"Where is the wonderful" (Ibid., 1807).

"My Father and" (Ibid., 469).

THOREAU, HENRY DAVID

"When God made man" (Witherell et al. *Henry D. Thoreau, Journal, Vol. I: 1837–1844*. Princeton: Princeton University Press, 1981, 375–76).

"Why, God, did you" (Ibid., 372).

"What if you" (Ibid., 373).

"I thank God" (Ibid., 400).

TOLSTOY, LEO

"Oh God, God" (Wilson, A. *Tolstoy*. London: Hamilton Press, 1988, 315).

"God and the soul" (Tolstoy, L. *Recollections and Essays*. London: Oxford University Press, 1937, 498).

"The longer we" (Tolstoy, L., "Patriotism, Slavery of Our Times," in *The Complete Work of L. Tolstoy*. New York: T. Y. Crowell Co., 1927, 165).

"Traditions may proceed" (Ibid., 164).

"Does truth cease" (Ibid., 302).

"There will be" (Ibid.).

"Yet another effort" (Ibid., 303).

"He has actually" (Ibid.).

"The solution before" (Ibid.).

"For life is life" (Ibid., 308).

"Each will have" (Ibid., 378).

WORDSWORTH, WILLIAM

"Glory to God" (Deutch, B. *Poetry Handbook*. New York: Funk and Wagnalls, 1957, 147).

"Stern Lawgiver!" (Dowden, E. *Poems by W. Wordsworth*. London: Gin and Co., 1897, 203).